The
Blood
of the
Moon

The Blood of the Moon

UNDERSTANDING THE HISTORIC STRUGGLE
BETWEEN ISLAM AND WESTERN CIVILIZATION

George Grant

THOMAS NELSON PUBLISHERS®
Nashville

A Division of Thomas Nelson, Inc.
www.ThomasNelson.com

Library of Congress Cataloging-in-Publication Data

Grant, George, 1954–
    The blood of the moon : understanding the historic struggle between Islam and Western civilization / George Grant.
        p. cm.
    "Revised and updated"
    Includes bibliographical references and index.
    ISBN 0-7852-6543-0 (pbk.)
    1. Middle East—Politics and government. 2. East and West. 3. Islam and politics. I. Title.
DS62 .G73 2002
956—dc21   2001056238

Printed in the United States of America

01 02 03 04 05 PHX 6 5 4 3 2

To my students at FCS and BC

who know the truth

To my yokefellows at CCC and MMC

who demonstrate the truth

And to the courageous men and women

in Operation Enduring Freedom

who defend the truth

Joyeuse Garde

Contents

Part Three
The Future and Faith

Introduction

You cannot escape the revelation of the identical by taking refuge in the illusion of the multiple.

—G. K. CHESTERTON[1]

When the awful specter of wars and rumors of wars grab the full attention of men and women the world over—wrenching us from our daily routines, our families, and our ongoing responsibilities—innumerable questions loom large in our minds: *Why? Why is this happening? Why is this happening now? Why is this happening to us?*

No single book can hope to fully answer such questions. No collection of facts, figures, and analyses, however well informed, can possibly grasp the full dimensions of man's inhumanity to man. Indeed, the remarkable Victorian preacher Charles Haddon Spurgeon once wrote, "I would have everybody able to read, and write, and cipher; indeed I don't think a man can know too much; but mark you, the knowing of these things is not education; and there are millions of your reading and writing people who are as ignorant as neighbor Norton's calf, that did not know its own mother."[2]

Even so, I am convinced that we can make substantial progress toward answering such questions when we are willing to look at the abundant lessons of the past. As Hilaire Belloc has said, "Time after time mankind is driven against the rocks of the horrid reality of a fallen creation. And time after time mankind must learn the hard lessons of history—the lessons that for some dangerous and awful reason we can't seem to keep in our collective memory."[3] This book is an attempt to recover some of that collective memory.

Originally written in the days leading up to the Gulf War in 1991, it has been thoroughly revised and updated to try to help all of us sort through the difficult issues that inevitably attach themselves to the perpetual tangle of conflicts and controversies of East-West relations. The structure of the study is thus fairly straightforward. Looking at the contemporary character of Islamic civilization and its clash with the Christian West actually demands a fairly comprehensive survey of all the great civilizations of antiquity from Egypt, Babylon, and Assyria to Persia, Greece, and Rome. Not surprisingly the story of the sudden appearance of Muhammad's ardent faith along Byzantium's frontier is also instructive. Likewise, a quick refresher course in such arcane subjects as the Crusades, colonialism, Inquisition, and Reconquesta provides us with helpful insights. The primordial enmity between the rival children of Abraham—between Ishmael, son of Hagar, and Isaac, son of Sarah; between Muslim and Jew; between the Arabs and Israel—is of significance. And the many good-intentioned attempts of the men and nations to resolve the grave dilemmas of the East-West clash—particularly those of the British, French, and Russians following World War I and the breakup of the Ottoman Empire—afford us with a vital perspective. In addition, a brief survey of the biblical view of global relations—beginning with the Tower of Babel and extending to the United Nations, the Gulf War, and the current global coalition to fight terrorism—is helpful in putting all the accumulated historical data into proper perspective.

In this new edition a bibliography is included for readers interested in further study, though it is offered with the caveat that the story of this East-West clash of cultures is far from complete and the number of resources is sure to greatly multiply in the days just ahead. A glossary is also provided. To say that the translation of Arabic words into Western languages is an inexact science is an understatement, at the very least. Even fairly common terms such as *Koran* may be variously rendered as *Qu'ran, Quran,* or *Ku'ron.* Likewise, the followers of Muhammad may be called *Muslims, Moslems,* or even *Muhammadans.* Even the name of the prophet is alternately spelled *Mohammed, Mohamet,* or *Muhammad.* I have generally chosen to follow the standard of the *International Herald Tribune*—the joint overseas publication of the *New York Times* and the *Washington Post.* Still, I felt the further explanation of a glossary would be helpful to the average reader.

Quotations from the *Koran* and the *Hadith* are taken from an English translation. That, in and of itself, is problematical. For one thing, Islamic tradition forbids the use of translation from the original autographs—inscribed in Classical Arabic—due to the very real possibility of textual corruption or theological presumption creeping into the manuscript. Thus, there is no definitive English translation, and the translations we generally have vary widely in both construction and interpretation of the original. Though I consulted several popular editions including the fine Penguin Classics translation by N. J. Dawood, I settled on a Christian Palestinian edition—translated by Seth Kajouri and published by St. Catherine's Publication Society in Bethlehem—for all citations in this book.

Although Middle Eastern politics has long been my chief academic interest, not being an academic has meant that this is the first book that I have had the opportunity to devote entirely to that subject. The temptation to make it a tediously footnoted treatise was quite strong. I tried my best to resist such pretensions for the sake of timeliness and accessibility. I wanted as many people as possible to have access to the information as soon as possible, so I rapidly put the manuscript together with an eye toward brevity. I am probably more aware than anyone of the limitations that a book like this inevitably has. I have opted purposefully for a cursory look at the issues, thus, the unashamedly slender volume you now hold.

Spurgeon excused the succinctness of one of his books by jesting: "If this were a regular sermon preached from a pulpit, of course, I should make it long and dismal, like a winter's night, for fear people should call me eccentric. As it is only meant to be read at home, I will make it short, though it will not be sweet, for I have not a sweet subject."[4]

The character of this present volume is, I pray, excused on the same grounds in the hope that others may one day be able to build on its foundations.

Deo soli Gloria. Jesu Juva.[5]

Part One

The Present and History

Allah has bought from the Umma—the true believers of Islam—their selves and their substance in return for Paradise; they fight in the way of Allah, killing and being killed. Their promise is written in the blood of the moon. Rejoice in the bargain. That is surely the supreme triumph.

—Koran 9:112

There was a great earthquake; and the sun became black as sackcloth made of hair, and the whole moon became like blood; and the stars of the sky fell to the earth, as a fig tree casts its unripe figs when shaken by a great wind. And the sky was split apart like a scroll when it is rolled up; and every mountain and island were moved out of their places. And the kings of the earth and the great men and the commanders and the rich and the strong and every slave and free man, hid themselves in the caves and among the rocks of the mountains; and they said to the mountains and to the rocks, "Fall on us and hide us from the presence of Him who sits on the throne, and from the wrath of the Lamb; for the great day of their wrath has come; and who is able to stand?"

—Revelation 6:12–17

1

Questions and Answers

The greatest advances in human civilization have come when we recovered what we had lost: when we learned the lessons of history.

—WINSTON CHURCHILL[1]

It seems that there are far more questions than answers. Despite the fact that our best experts have devoted hundreds of thousands of words, millions of man-hours, and billions of dollars to unravel the snarl of mystery that surrounds the current East-West conflict, most of us are as confounded as ever. And our questions only seem to multiply.

Just two weeks before the most brazen and horrific terrorist attacks in human history were carried out on the Pentagon in Washington, D.C., and the World Trade Center in New York City, the *Mufti* of Jerusalem, Sheik Ekrima Sobri, offered a chillingly prophetic prayer in the Al Aqsa mosque:

Allah, there is no strength but your strength. Destroy, therefore, the Zionist occupation and its helpers and its agents. Destroy the U.S. and its helpers and its agents. Destroy Britain and its helpers and its agents. Prepare those who will soon unite the Muslims of the world and march in the footsteps of Saladin. Allah, we ask you for forgiveness, forgiveness before death, and mercy and forgiveness after death. Allah, grant victory to Islam and the Muslims in the coming war.[2]

A host of questions immediately spring to mind: What did the supreme spiritual leader of Palestinian Muslims know, and when did he know it? What war is he talking about? Why would he invoke such virulent hatred against the Western world? Why would he pronounce such fierce anathemas against the nations most responsible for brokering peace between his own people and the Israelis? Why would he reserve such impious enmity for the powers that had ensured the transformation of Yasser Arafat from a rogue terrorist operative into a respected nationalist leader and his Palestine Liberation Organization from a disreputable revolutionary cell into a legitimate regional government? Why would he so openly attack his land's chief financial and political patrons? In short, how did we become the enemy in his unholy *Ji'had?*

And there are still more questions.

The four commercial airliners that were hijacked early in the morning of September 11, 2001, were transformed into weapons of mass destruction by a handful of men willing to lay down their lives as martyrs for their faith. America, indeed, most of the Western world, was utterly shocked. But why? Were we not given abundant warning that such unimaginably ignoble deeds might actually be forthcoming? What did we learn from the appalling suicide bombings that rocked Israel week after week during the previous year, or the suicide attack on the U.S. destroyer *Cole* in a Yemen harbor in October 2000, or the suicide bombing of the

U.S. Embassies in Kenya and Tanzania in August 1998, or the suicide attack on the U.S. Army barracks, the Saudi Khobar Towers, in 1996? Why were we so surprised? More, why were the military, security, and intelligence communities so surprised?

Even that does not exhaust our questions.

Saudi exile Osama bin Laden has been the locus of international terrorism for more than a decade. His network of confederated revolutionary cells, Al Qaeda, was established in 1988 and funded by the vast and diverse fortune he inherited from his family. In the years since, members of Al Qaeda have repeatedly struck U.S. and Israeli targets and have destabilized moderate regimes the world over. In 1990, they assassinated Rabbi Meir Kahane in a midtown Manhattan hotel. In 1992, they bombed American troops stationed in Yemen during the Gulf War demobilization. In 1993, they shot down U.S. helicopters over Somalia. A month later, they set off a massive explosion in the underground garage of the World Trade Center in New York. In 1994, they unleashed a wave of terror against India in Kashmir and genocide against Copts in Egypt. In 1995, they deployed terrorist cells in the Philippines, Malaysia, and Indonesia where assassinations, insurrections, and kidnappings became a regular occurrence. In 1996, they not only attacked U.S. military housing facilities in Dhaharan, but they launched radical new revolutionary movements in Chechnya, East Timor, Chad, Sudan, Nigeria, Pakistan, and Algeria. In 1998, they issued a *fatwah* in conjunction with other notorious terrorist organizations such as the Egyptian Al Gama'a Al Islam, the Palestinian Hamas, the Lebanese Hezbollah, the Pakistani Jamaat'i Islam, and the Yemeni Al Ji'had. The spiritual decree asserted the "duty of all Muslims to kill U.S. citizens, civilian and military, and their allies everywhere."[3] Though the Clinton administration targeted Al

Qaeda operations in Afghanistan and Sudan with surgical military strikes and placed Osama on the FBI's "most wanted" list, little was actually done to stymie their efforts in London, Paris, Hamburg, and indeed, in schools, communities, and airports all across the U.S. How is this possible? How can an organization with such a sordid past be free to continue to pursue its pernicious goals?

There are yet more questions.

A decade ago three countries in the strife-riven Middle East were invaded by neighboring nations within a matter of a few weeks. Their governments were displaced, their people were dispossessed, and their resources were dissipated. When Syria overran Lebanon, the world barely noticed. When Libya led a coup in Chad, the incident was almost entirely overlooked. But when Iraq swept into Kuwait, an international crisis—and ultimately the Gulf War—was provoked. Why? What made the difference? Iraq's antics in the region were not exactly unprecedented. The conflict between Kuwait and Iraq has flared up again and again over the past thirty years, resulting in armed confrontation on at least five occasions. In 1961 and again in 1973, Iraq actually annexed portions of its tiny gulf neighbor. Why, then, was the intelligence community in the United States so surprised when the old rivalry resurfaced in 1990? And why the dramatic reaction?

Still more questions arise.

Throughout 2001, world attention was focused on the newly reinvigorated Palestinian resistance movement, or *Intifada*, in Israel's occupied West Bank and Gaza territories. Contrasting images of the Jewish victims of terror attacks on pizza parlors and of the Palestinian victims of Israeli retaliation have been etched in the minds of television viewers around the globe.

Meanwhile, innumerable other Islamic *Intifadas* across the region are virtually ignored—the *Intifada* of the Kurds in Iraq, the *Intifada* of the Shi'ites in Tajukskaya, the *Intifada* of the Albanian Muslims in Kosovo, the *Intifada* of the Druze in Lebanon, the *Intifada* of the Azaria in Azerbaijan, the *Intifada* of the Sunnu in Kashmir, and the *Intifada* of the Dra'hanna in Sudan. Why is one uprising front-page news when all the others constitute no news at all?

Even now, our questions continue to present themselves.

In Iran, the home of Islamic fundamentalism, the excavation and restoration of the ancient ruins of pagan Persia have become a national priority. Likewise, in Syria, Iraq, Saudi Arabia, Algeria, Libya, Jordan, and Egypt—each a very strict Muslim state—the artifacts and achievements of their pre-Muslim forebears have become rallying points for both national patriotism and pan-Arab pride. Why this apparent lapse of piety and consistency?

The slippery, difficult, and discomfiting questions just keep coming. Like the conflict that engendered them, there seems to be no end to them.

So, where can we turn for answers?

By now it is fairly clear that the answers will not be found in State Department dossiers. Neither will they be disclosed in classified Pentagon reports. They are not likely to be revealed in official press briefings. And they certainly will not be related in the dispatches of the popular media.

Perhaps the best place to start looking for answers is not tomorrow's newspaper, but yesterday's history books. It may well be that insights into a whole host of the plaguing dilemmas of both the present and the foreseeable future may be discerned best as we carefully study the events of the past. The elusive answers to our thorniest questions may only begin to be divulged as we familiarize ourselves with when, where, how, and why those questions arose in the first place.

Review As Preview

"History is bunk."[4] When Henry Ford said that, he was not only stating an opinion about his least favorite subject in school; he was expressing an American state of mind. We are not particularly fond of the musty, dusty past. And whatever fascinations we may continue to harbor, we relegate to the realms of sentiment or nostalgia. As William Shakespeare memorably asserted, we tend to believe that the record of events long past is as relevant to our lives as "a tale told by an idiot, full of sound and fury, signifying nothing."[5] Or as Guy de Maupassant said, we are prone to think of history as little more than a "dust heap."[6]

The renowned historian Daniel Boorstin has pointed out:

> In our schools today, the story of our nation has been replaced by *social studies*—which is the study of what ails us *now*. In our churches, the effort to see the essential nature of man has been displaced by the *social gospel*—which is the polemic against the pet vices of *today*. Our book publishers no longer seek the timeless and the durable, but spend most of their efforts in a fruitless search for *la mode social commentary*—which they pray will not be out of age when the item goes to press. Our merchandisers frantically devise their New Year models, which will cease to be voguish when their sequels appear three months hence. Neither our classroom lessons nor our sermons nor our books nor the things we live with nor the houses we live in are any longer strong ties to our past.[7]

The result, according to Boorstin, is that "we have become a nation of short-term doomsayers. In a word, we have lost our sense of history. Without the materials of historical comparison, we are left with nothing but abstractions."[8]

It seems that in our mad rush toward progress and prosperity, we have become afflicted with a malignant contemporaneity. We don't really have time or patience to ponder the lessons of our legacy. We are too busy with the present to bother much with the past. As a result of this morbid preoccupation with ourselves, and its resulting historical ambivalence, if not ignorance, we have virtually locked ourselves into a recalcitrant present.

Thus, the English author and lecturer John H. Y. Briggs has poignantly argued that a historical awareness is essential for the health and well-being of any society; it enables us to know who we are, why we are here, and what we should do. He says, "Just as a loss of memory in an individual is a psychiatric defect calling for medical treatment, so too any community which has no social memory is suffering from an illness."[9]

Lord Acton, the great historian from the previous generation, made the same point, saying: "History must be our deliverer not only from the undue influence of other times, but from the undue influence of our own, from the tyranny of the environment and the pressures of the air we breathe."[10] The venerable aphorism remains as true today as ever: "He who forgets his own history is condemned to repeat it."[11]

The fact is, history is not just the concern of historians and social scientists. It is not the lonely domain of political prognosticators and ivory tower academics. It is the very stuff of life.

In the volatile, headline-grabbing conflict between Islam and the West, for instance, the importance of history ought to be obvious to even the most casual observer. Not only is the region steeped in glorious traditions that reach back to the very dawning of civilization, but more often than not, it is still governed by those ancient ambitions and rivalries. Islamic fundamentalists have seen the application or misapplication of American foreign policy through the lens of the medieval Crusades; Israelis have tenaciously held on to the occupied territories of the West Bank not only because of security concerns but also because of promises made millennia ago to the patriarch Abraham; Iraqis invaded the lands of fellow Muslims in Kuwait, Iran, and Kurdistan to settle grudges that date back to the time of Nebuchadnezzar; Iranians have stirred up revolutionary passions that have lain dormant since the demise of Ali and Hussein late in the seventh century; and Egyptians, recalling the former glory of pharaohs and pyramids, have issued calls for a revitalized military and a pan-Arab revival of their former empire.

The conflict between the cultures of the largely Islamic East and the largely Christian West is, of course, terribly complex. It involves questions of geopolitical security, economic development, market globalization, national sovereignty, racial rancor, religious contention, imperial ambition, and military prowess. But central to each of these questions is the primordial importance of history. Even the question of prophetic fulfillment revolves around various and sundry historical concerns. After all, the prophetic passages of the Bible are inextricably linked to the peoples, issues, and events of those ancient times when they were first recorded under the superintendence of our sovereign God. Prophecy is, in fact, *history foretold*—utilizing the same structure, language, and facility of *history retold*.

In addition, biblical prophecy is almost always fulfilled in three different ways across the span of time. There will be an initial fulfillment. There will be an ongoing fulfillment. And there will be an ultimate fulfillment. Therefore, understanding how prophecy *has been* fulfilled before is the most important key to understanding how prophecy *will be* fulfilled yet.

There can be little doubt, then, that understanding the past is the key to understanding the future. Especially when it comes to the conflict between Islam and the West, to ignore history is to invite disaster.

The Bible heavily emphasizes historical awareness—not at all surprising considering that the vast proportion of its own contents records the dealings of God with men and nations throughout the ages. Again and again in the Scriptures, God calls on His people to remember. He calls on us to remember the bondage, oppression, and deliverance of Egypt (Ex. 13:3; Deut. 6:20–23). He calls on us to remember the splendor, strength, and devotion of the Davidic kingdom (1 Chron. 16:8–36). He calls on us to remember the valor, forthrightness, and holiness of the prophets (James 5:7–11). He calls on us to remember the glories of creation (Ps. 104:1–30), the devastation of the Flood (2 Peter 2:4–11), the judgment of the great apostasies (Jude 5–11), the miraculous events of the Exodus (Deut. 5:15), the anguish of the desert wanderings (Deut. 8:1–6), the grief of the Babylonian exile (Ps. 137:1–6), the responsibility of the restoration (Ezra 9:5–15), the sanctity of the Lord's Day (Ex. 20:8), the graciousness of the commandments (Num. 15:39–40), and the ultimate victory of the Cross (1 Cor. 11:23–26). He calls on us to remember the lives and witnesses of all those who have gone before us in faith—forefathers, fathers, patriarchs, prophets, apostles, preachers, evangelists, martyrs, confessors, ascetics, and every righteous spirit made pure in Christ (1 Cor. 10:1–11; Heb. 11:3–40).

God calls on us to remember. As the psalmist has said,

> I shall remember the deeds of the LORD;
> Surely I will remember Thy wonders of old.
> I will meditate on all Thy work,
> And muse on Thy deeds.
> Thy way, O God, is holy;
> What god is great like our God?
> Thou art the God who workest wonders;
> Thou hast made known Thy strength among the peoples.
> Thou hast by Thy power redeemed Thy people,
> The sons of Jacob and Joseph. (Ps. 77:11–15)

> Oh give thanks to the LORD, call upon His name;
> Make known His deeds among the peoples.
> Sing to Him, sing praises to Him;
> Speak of all His wonders.
> Glory in His holy name;
> Let the heart of those who seek the LORD be glad.
> Seek the LORD and His strength;
> Seek His face continually.
> Remember His wonders which He has done,
> His marvels and the judgments uttered by His mouth.
>   (Ps. 105:1–5)

When Moses stood before the Israelites at the end of his long life, he did not exhort them with polemics or moralisms. He reminded them of the works of God in history. He reminded them of their duty to remember (Deut. 32:1–43).

When David stood before his family and friends following a great deliverance from his enemies, he did not stir them with sentiment or nostalgia. He reminded them of the works of God in history in a psalm of praise. He reminded them of their duty to remember (2 Sam. 22:1–51).

When Solomon stood before his subjects at the dedication of the newly constructed temple, he did not challenge them with logic or rhetoric. He simply reminded them of the works of God in history in a hymn of wisdom. He reminded them of their duty to remember (1 Kings 8:15–61).

When Nehemiah stood before the families of Jerusalem at the consecration of the rebuilt city walls, he did not bombard them with theology or theatrics. He reminded them of the works of God in history in a song of the covenant. He reminded them of their duty to remember (Neh. 9:9–38).

When Stephen stood before an accusing and enraged Sanhedrin, he did not confront them with apology or condemnation. He reminded them of the works of God in history in a litany of faith. He reminded them of their duty to remember (Acts 7:2–53).

Remembrance and forgetfulness are the measuring rods of faithfulness throughout the entire canon of Scripture. A family that passes its legacy on to its children will bear great fruit (Deut. 8:2–10). A family that fails to take its heritage seriously will remain barren (Deut. 8:11–14). A people that remembers the mighty deeds of the Lord will be blessed (Deut. 8:18). A people that forgets is doomed to frustration and failure (Deut. 8:19–20). In fact, the whole direction of a culture depends on the gracious appointments of memory:

Will Thy wonders be made known in the darkness?
And Thy righteousness in the land of forgetfulness?
   (Ps. 88:12)

That is why the Bible makes it plain that there are only two
kinds of people in the world: effectual doers and forgetful hearers
(James 1:25). And that is why the ministry of the Holy Spirit in
the lives of believers is primarily to bring to our remembrance the
word of truth (John 14:26).

Philip Schaff, the prolific church historian during the previous
generation, argued stridently that we must be eternally vigilant in
the task of handing on our great legacy—to remember and then
to inculcate that remembrance in the hearts and minds of our
children:

> How shall we labor with any effect to build up the church, if we
> have no thorough knowledge of its history, or fail to apprehend it
> from the proper point of observation? History is, and must ever
> continue to be, next to God's Word, the richest foundation of
> wisdom, and the surest guide to all successful practical activity.[12]

If we are to negotiate the dangerous shoals of Middle Eastern
diplomacy with any degree of success, we cannot simply match
our adversaries, army for army and missile for missile. We cannot
responsibly hope to bring resolve to eons-old conflicts if we do
not comprehend their roots. David R. Carlin said,

> The best way to develop an attitude of responsibility toward the
> future is to cultivate a sense of responsibility toward the past. We
> are born into a world that we didn't make, and it is only fair that

we should be grateful to those who did make it. Such gratitude carries with it the imperative that we preserve and at least slightly improve the world that has been given us before passing it on to subsequent generations. We stand in the midst of many generations. If we are indifferent to those who went before us and actually existed, how can we expect to be concerned for the well-being of those who come after us and only potentially exist?[13]

His Story

Not only is it perilously imprudent to ignore history, but it is equally imprudent to ignore the hand of God in shaping it. Even a wrinkle in time bears the obvious impress of God's own good providence. Alas, you could hardly tell that by looking at the average history textbook these days, though. If history is, as Stephen Mansfield has quipped, "More than dates and dead people," you would never know it based on most of the printed evidence.[14] Modern historians can agree on very few things. But when it comes to God, there is sudden consensus. The long-held notion that history is His story is fiercely resisted in our day.

But history is full of the indecipherable mysteries of Providence, and any attempt to reduce the process of its legends, epics, movements, heroes, and villains to a mere mechanical or material science is destined to be more than a little ridiculous—as the sad legacies of Karl Marx, Arnold Toynbee, H. G. Wells, and Woodrow Wilson have proved.

It is true that certain undeniably fixed milestones emerge—such as the Battles of Hastings and Waterloo, the regicides of Louis XVI and Charles I, the triumphs of Bismarck and Richelieu, and the tragedies of the Hapsburgs and Hohenstaufens—and you can, from them, build up certain vague rules regarding the onward march of civilization. But for the most part, the events of history have the habit of coming up out of nothing, like the little particles of ice that float to the surface of the Seine at the beginning of a frost, or like the little oak trees that crop up everywhere in the broad fields of East Sussex. They arise silently and unpredictably.

And that surprises us. It is too easy for us to forget—or to try to ignore—the fact that the doings of man are on the knees of an inscrutable and sovereign God.

One of the most important and most neglected aspects of His story called history is that the story is not yet complete and will not be until providence has run its resolute course. We can truly comprehend the events of the past only when we recognize them as part and parcel of the ethical outworking of God's plan for the present and even for the future.

The irony of this concept is so large that it may be too large to be seen. Thus, the writing and rewriting of history are often little more than the material preferences and prejudices of one age gazing into a distant mirror of another age.

Modern secular historians are especially prone to fall into this alluring trap. And so, they quixotically rail against the upstart evils of today by lambasting the tenured virtues of yesterday. They attempt to impose sanctions against some unacceptable form of behavior by instituting a kind of retroactive apartheid. It is the same odd impulse that induces certain politicians to attempt to cure the ills of Timbuktu by starting an agitation in Tulsa or to reform the administration of Montevideo by holding a referendum in Minneapolis.

The aim of this book is quite simple: to shed a little light on the perilous present and the frightening future by shedding a little light on the providential past. I have not tried to plot either a diplomatic or a military solution to this current crisis. I have not tried to decode the prophetic destiny of the men and nations involved. I have only attempted to remind us of some long-forgotten facts of history—to expose the roots of the crisis. I can only hope that, in the process, I will be able to help provoke a new attitude of responsibility—and to help us avoid the disaster that always awaits the oblivious.

Chapter Two

The Eleventh Plague

The funeral sermon of the chivalry of Christendom has been preached so many times that most people probably thought it had already been interred. But horrific inhumanity of modernity's humanism has served as a kind of benevolent cataclysm which shattered the smothering uniformity of contemporary barbarism, and once again, it seems, civilization may be seen as an option by thinking men and women. Ever hopeful, the phoenix of chivalry may yet rise from the ashes of this misbegotten wreckage we call modern pop culture.

—TRISTAN GYLBERD[1]

The historic conflict between Islam and Western civilization is not a theoretical notion—cold, impersonal, and distant. It is a reality woven into the fabric of the personal lives of men, women, and children across the world. It affects real people, real families, striving to fulfill real hopes and dreams in real communities. It is best understood in terms of their real stories.

As tens of thousands of Americans watched on television with a sense of surreal horror, the two towers of the World Trade Center collapsed into flaming steel, rubble, and dust, and vanished from the skyline of lower Manhattan. By that time Katherine Ilachinski, a seventy-year-old architect, had already made her way out of the financial district, navigated the panicked streets toward Chinatown, and was walking across the Manhattan bridge. As a girl, she survived the German bombing of Belgrade, but she admitted she had never endured anything quite like this before.

She began the morning in her office on the ninety-first floor of Two World Trade Center, working on a sketch for a renovation project at an electrical substation at the Hoboken terminal of New Jersey Transit. That was when the first hijacked jet hit One World Trade just above the level of her office window.

"There was an explosion, and a fireball went along the side of my building where I was sitting," she later recalled. "It was so hot. It was like being in a boiler. I had to get out of my office. I went into an interior passage, then into the main corridor, to the elevators. You know, I was in the building in 1993, when we were bombed, and that time my instincts were completely different. Then, I closed my office. This time, I just wanted to get out of the building. Some people were taking the stairs. But I thought, I'm too old to walk so far down."[2] She took the first elevator she could. It descended only to the seventy-eighth floor. The lobby there was mobbed, everybody trying to get in the elevators to the ground. It was still too high for her to try to walk, but the elevators to the ground were so crowded, she was unable to squeeze through. She decided to take a relatively empty intermediate elevator to the forty-fourth floor. But the scene in the lobby on forty-four was a repetition of seventy-eight. It was mobbed with people waiting for the elevator to the ground.

That was when Mrs. Ilachinski decided to try to walk down the north stairs. In the stairwell, she heard several announcements on the loudspeakers, saying that the building was safe, that there was no need for panic, and that workers should return to their offices. Nevertheless, she kept going. "I was just going down, down, down, like an automaton."³ A few moments later, after the second hijacked plane crashed into the building, there were no more announcements.

On her way out into the courtyard of the massive World Trade Center Plaza, Mrs. Ilachinski passed several firemen rushing into the building. Their bravery—and their terrible losses—quickly became emblematic of American heroism. More than three hundred firemen were killed trying to rescue their fellow New Yorkers; the dead included Chief of Department Peter Ganci, First Deputy Fire Commissioner William Feehan, and a department chaplain, a Franciscan friar named Mychal Judge. Three elite units—Rescues 1, 2, and 4—appeared to be entirely wiped out. "The Fire Department will recover, but I don't know how," Fire Commissioner Thomas Von Essen told reporters.⁴ As one building after another collapsed, the Office of Emergency Management had to repeatedly seek out new command centers. The firefighters finally ended up working out of a firehouse north of ground zero on Houston Street, in Greenwich Village.

Over the course of the next several hours, days, and weeks, the firefighters became the galvanizing image of a grieving nation steeling its resolve for the difficult task of going forward. Entertainers, professional sports teams, politicians, and average Americans from every walk of life would don T-shirts and ball caps emblazoned with the now familiar FDNY.

For Janine Smith and her three young children, such tokens of respect and inspiration offer only a little consolation. "People tell me my husband died a hero," she lamented. "And I know that should somehow make it easier for me. But it doesn't. It just doesn't."

By any measure, Jonathan Smith was a hero. The veteran rescue worker, heedless of the grave danger he faced, plunged into the chaos of the crippled World Trade Center towers in the hope of saving the men and women trapped inside. He had just entered the lobby when he was suddenly engulfed in the collapsing hulk of pulverized concrete and twisted steel. He has not been seen since.

In her grief, Janine is not thinking of medals, posthumous honors, or flag-waving celebrations. "I am not up nights thinking that he died a hero. I'm up nights just thinking that he died."[5]

Like man himself, the arid crescent of land where East meets West in the Middle East is an enigma. The cradle of civilization, the wellspring of faith, the powder keg of ardor, and the terminus of time—there is no other place on earth where so much has occurred for so long and affected so many. The rugged swath of sand and stone east of the Mediterranean is the ominous, swarthy, and mysterious hinge upon which, it seems, all of history turns. Alternately rocked by unending wars and soothed by undying devotion, tortured by unflinching fanaticism and calmed by unyielding patience, this small crescent of sand and stone is once again the stage upon which the passion play of mankind's trauma is set—where war is waged for the sake of peace, where hatred is stoked for the sake of righteousness, and where tyranny is invoked for the sake of freedom.

The swirling dust clouds just above the surface of the desert give the amber lamps of military caravans the gauzy glow of distant planets. The long lines of men and armaments are hardly an uncommon sight here. Before American troops had ever established their bivouacs, the British, the French, the Turks, the Saracens, the Crusaders, the Mongols, the Greeks, the Romans, the Byzantines, the Persians, the Egyptians, the Sumerians, the Babylonians, and the Assyrians had also passed this way. Even so, the landscape has never lost its ethereal and unearthly look. This ancient bridge between the two worlds of East and West—common to every resurgent ambition—is yet alien to man. And so it shall ever be.

"You really feel your mortality here," Mark Edwards told me. Stationed in the Saudi desert near Riyadh, Mark was a part of the first wave of troops sent in to face down the aggression of Saddam Hussein during the Gulf War. "Just north of here, Alexander the Great confronted Darius in 331 B.C. Over to the west, Saladin met Richard the Lionhearted in A.D. 1191. Just over the horizon there, Napoleon was turned back by Laraturk in 1798. They've all come and gone. And the desert wind and the passing time have covered their tracks without a trace. It's almost as if they had never been here at all. Now here we are, in the same place, fighting the same battles for the same reasons."

He looked across the vast expanse of sandy crags and then shrugged in resignation. "But then, what's a guy gonna do? I'm in the Reserves because I want to serve my country. So I don't take my duty lightly. But I'll tell you, it was hard saying good-bye to my wife and children. Really hard. This was our daughter's first

Christmas. We'd moved into a new neighborhood. I'd just gotten promoted to supervisor at the plant. Things really seemed to be going well for us. And then this."

He told me about several of the men he had met in the camp—men who, like Mark, had left homes and families, jobs, hopes, and dreams to come to this faraway alien land to rid the world of the scourge of tyranny and terror. "Each of us is ready to fight," he said. "And we're quite confident we can win. Hands down. But we can't help but wonder why—and if it'll make any difference. I guess those are the questions that come up in any war. And there is nothing we can do—win, lose, or draw—about the desert wind or the passing of time. Nothing except pray."

Then with wry irony in his voice, he added, "The problem is, we can't even pray all that often for fear of offending the Saudis."

The poet William Blake first gave the name *Jerusalem* to all that was tender and lovely in the human soul. He wrote of her as a beautiful woman who maintains her virtue despite the indignities imposed by the ages. He described her as a pristine kingdom whose true spirit has fallen asleep but will not die, despite the decline of man and his ignominious fall. Blake's vivid poetic prescience grasped the truth that this city, more than any other, has always paradigmatically nourished sincere holiness—and sincere betrayal.

Here, where the present is but a gossamer above ages past, history is inescapable. It hangs in the air like the wail of the faithful before the Western Wall. It intrudes on every conversation like the wheedling cries of Arab merchants at the Jaffa Gate. It pierces every waking moment like the glinting gold of the *Haram es Sherif* against the Judean sky.

And yet the gossamer is thick and dull.

"The past is the air that we breathe and the hope that we cling to," Uldi Salreageini told me. "But the present is the awful necessity that we must live with—holy places guarded with automatic weapons, ancient relics marred by political posturing, centuries-old streets with security police careening along in armored vehicles, and the quietude of prayer disturbed by the wail of sirens and the angry cries of the *Intifada*'s terror. Such things ought not to be. But alas, so it has been throughout time. Someone has said that the constant presence of strife and the threat of terror are not interruptions of Jerusalem's historical charm—they *are* Jerusalem's historical charm. Still, they are more than a little disturbing."

To emerge from the architectural and acoustical marvels within the Church of Saint Anne, built by the Crusaders just adjacent to the five porticoes of the Pool of Bethesda, only to be confronted with Uzi-bearing soldiers is indeed discomfiting and disorienting. To pray in the Church of the Holy Sepulcher before Golgotha under the watchful eyes of security police with walkie-talkies is likewise a strange anomaly. To wander down the Via Dolorosa recalling the chronology of the gospel accounts of the passion of Christ Jesus, with the angry anarchy of the Palestinians' Saracen Quarter as a backdrop, is surely somehow misplaced and misbegotten.

But then, that is Jerusalem as much as the glorious view from the Mount of Olives or the dust swirling through the crowded streets along the Kidron Valley, as much as the quietude of Gordon's Garden Tomb or the frenzied bustle around the Damascus Gate, as much as the quiet intensity of *Shabat* or the tense solemnity of Ramadan.

"We came here for a taste of peace," Uldi told me. "But we have supped only on war. I myself have fought in every war since 1948. My sons fought in 1973. Now my grandchildren are in the military. Last month, all three generations served together in exercises in the Golan Heights. Can you believe it? An old man and his grandchildren serving together in war?"

Flipping open his small, worn copy of the Torah, he showed me the place where Moses promised the people of the covenant that they would never again be afflicted by the diseases and plagues of Egypt if only they would obey the Lord in every detail of their lives. "Some say that this plague of continual violence and upheaval, worse than all of the ten that afflicted Egypt, is our recompense for unrighteousness. The judgment of Jehovah."

He turned to me with tears streaking his leathery brown cheeks. "I don't believe that, of course. I just wish the madness could end. I just wish that this eleventh plague would pass. Somewhere. Some way. Sometime. I am tired. We are all. Pray for the peace of Jerusalem. Won't you?"

☾

"We are in a no-win situation," Michael al Jerash told me. "Truly we are between a rock and a hard place. The rock is pan-Arab Islam. The hard place is the West. If we please one, we alienate the other. If we straddle the line between the two, we will be crushed by both. No matter where the battle lines are drawn, we will be caught in the middle. We will lose. That is the dilemma of Jordan in general—and of Arab Christians here in particular."

His piercing Bedouin eyes scanned the scene in front of him—one of the many lively *Souqs* not far from the fabled Qasr Khareneh Citadel. The marketplace was a warren of alleyways filled with the frantic clutter of merchants hawking their wares—intricate *narguilah* pipes; copper-studded *zanzibarz* chests; tall, exotic *hookahs;* richly embroidered *khaimah* textiles; ornate *hufuf* pottery; jewel-encrusted *khanjar* knives; antique *dillah* coffee pots; and deep iron *mihmahs* skillets.

"My family first came here from Cilicia at the beginning of the second century," he said. "The Roman settlement—which was at that time called Philadelphia—had a dynamic Christian community that, according to our tradition, was the recipient of Saint John's sole gracious pastoral letter in all of the Apocalypsion. My forefathers lived as a persecuted minority under the successive rules of the Byzantines, the Sassanids, the Umayyads, the Saljuks, the Ottomans, the British, and now the Hashemites. But this most recent threat is the gravest of all."

As we walked toward *Jebel al Qalat*, the harsh noon sun, like muted moonlight, put to sleep the colors. There were only bright splashes of light and deep, foreboding shadows. The streets became a monochromatic maze. "Our region has been anything but stable in recent years," he said. "King Abdullah was assassinated in 1951. King Talal was forced to abdicate a little more than a year later. And King Hussein has suffered at least five attempts on his life and three concerted coups. But with the constriction we face today, there is really no telling how, or if, we will be able to survive. And we Christians are likely to suffer the brunt of whatever scenario plays its course here. We are the forgotten element of this whole dilemma."

He stopped and asked, as much to himself as to me, "Do you

think the church in the West will remember us? Is there any ground for hope? Or will war swallow us up once again?"

The woman on the other end of the phone line was agitated. She told me that the trouble had begun in church—which is, of course, a profound assessment of both historical and biblical theology. After some time, the whole story came out.

"Clearly we are in the last days," the guest speaker at her church had said. "The signs of the times are indisputable. Jesus is coming soon. We can expect to see the rapture of the church, the Great Tribulation, the mark of the Beast, the reign of the Antichrist, the revival of the Roman Empire, the Battle of Armageddon, and the initiation of the Millennium—all within this very generation."

His eloquence held the congregation in rapt attention. With authority he quoted supporting verses, spouted vital statistics, and reiterated significant dates. He referred to maps, charts, slides, and time lines, all luminously projected on the screen behind the pulpit. For more than an hour he explained how the events currently splashed across the world's headlines were specifically predicted in the Bible thousands of years before.

And he was a man to be believed. He was an expert on the subject of prophecy, after all—a tenured professor at one of the most respected evangelical seminaries in America.

Even so, after the service the congregation was abuzz. In this town, where several thousand troops had been stationed until the military buildup in the distant desert lands of the East, any discussion of the conflict between Islam and the West was certain to stoke the fires of interest and concern. Out in the parking lot, the wives and children, the parents and loved ones, and the friends and neighbors of those who had been called up and deployed mulled over the implications of the sermon in tense knots of conversation.

"I have to tell you, I'm more confused than ever," one man volunteered in frustration. "All this business about killer bees and Cobra helicopters is a bit much for me."

"Well, it's a matter of interpretation really," answered another. "You have to know what to look for—how to decipher Scripture's ancient poetic imagery."

"I know. But I've been hearing this stuff all my life. The same charts. The same maps. The same scenarios. Only the dates change. They keep having to push them back. It just gets more and more inconclusive as the years roll on, and the system gets more and more convoluted. Always doomsaying."

"But the Bible says . . ."

"No, now, don't get me wrong. I'm not questioning the Bible. Not at all. But you said yourself that it's all a matter of interpretation. I just have to wonder if we're not kind of baptizing the headlines onto the Bible instead of the other way around. This sort of speculation may be suitable for potboiler novels, but I've got to question its practicality in times like these."

"All I know or care about is that my husband is right in the middle of what may or may not be an awful conflagration with ruthless terrorists," a young mother interjected. "I'm not sure how relevant speculative pop prophecy is to me and my children right now. I'm just trying to walk with Christ moment by moment—to keep our heads above water and our family functioning. I'm looking to the Scriptures for wisdom and direction as well as for comfort."

"I don't know if these are the end times," responded another. "But I'm not so sure it really matters. I do know that God is sovereign and that He's given us a job to do. Whether there are hitchhiking angels in southern California or Beast-coded Social Security checks in New Hampshire or demon-controlled master computers in Belgium is another matter altogether. The Bible informs us so that we can do what God wants us to do and we can be what He wants us to be."

"Well, I'm not sure what to believe either," said still another. "I can't decide whether I should be terrified or excited. I think I'm just confused."

"I just wish I understood better why all this is happening right now and how the Bible applies—without the spectacularization," the first man said. "I'd like to know why my son's life is on the line right now."

"Amen to that," the others concurred.

☾

Monday night football at the Meadowlands: for longtime fan Kevin Tamirelli, there was hardly anything in life that he enjoyed better. But just two weeks after the terrorist strikes, he found little to enjoy as he sat in his regular seat near the corner of the north end zone. And it wasn't that his beloved Jets were beaten by San Francisco in a close, hard-fought contest. "My wife made me come. She thought that it would help me get back to life as usual. But, I think maybe it is still just too soon."[6]

As he looked around the stadium, with flags waving, fans cheering, and music blaring, he could still only think about the tragedy. A tragedy that had struck all around him. He lost his best friend since high school in the World Trade Center. "For a game like this, he would be the one sitting right here next to me." He lost a very dear and close cousin in the Pentagon. "We grew up together." He lost his boss on one of the planes from Boston's Logan Airport. "He was a fighter. I know he didn't go down quietly." And he lost all of his buddies and peers from Cantor Fitzgerald, the bond trading firm where he had worked until just recently. "They tell me two-thirds of the staff is unaccounted for and presumed dead. Guys I had worked with for years. Moms and dads and brothers and sisters and sons and daughters. I can't even begin to grasp it all."[7]

Like so many others, Kevin had been walking around as if in a daze. "It has all been so surreal." He was feeling guilty. Angry. Helpless. And even a little afraid. "Sometimes I think I'm just being melodramatic. I try to talk myself into getting on with life. I try to convince myself that if I cave in to these emotions, I'm handing the victory over to the terrorists. But then a wave of despair sweeps over me. Everyone says time will heal. I don't know. I'm beginning to think that maybe I'm going to need something more than just time."[8]

Just then the Jets made a long gain—a beautiful lofting pass across the length of the field by quarterback Vinny Testaverde. The crowd roared. Kevin barely noticed. His mind was somewhere else entirely, obsessed with the blood of the moon.

Part Two

The Past and Prophecy

I am the wound and the knife. I am the blow and the cheek. I am the limbs and the wheel. I am the victim and the executioner.

—Les Fleurs du Mal[1]

I will show wonders in the heavens and in the earth:
Blood and fire and pillars of smoke.
The sun shall be turned into darkness,
And the moon into blood,
Before the coming of the great and awesome day of the Lord.
And it shall come to pass
That whoever calls on the name of the Lord
Shall be saved.

—Joel 2:30–32 nkjv

Chapter Three

A Simple Faith

Oh, East is East, and West is West, and never the twain shall meet,
Till earth and sky stand presently at God's great judgment seat.
—RUDYARD KIPLING[1]

Islam showed the world two very different faces in the hours and days immediately following the terrorist attacks on Washington, D.C., and New York. The contrast caused a great deal of confusion and consternation throughout the Western world. On the one hand, commentators, experts, clerics, and statesmen went out of their way to assure us that Islam was peaceful, that the terrorists did not represent the faith of Muhammad, and that all true Muslims were as horrified as everyone else at the attack. On the other hand, ordinary Muslims everywhere seemed to belie that sense of certainty and assurance in both word and deed.

Shortly after the news of the unfolding horrors at the Pentagon and the World Trade Center was first beamed around the world by global media outlets like CNN, Sky News, and the BBC, spontaneous celebrations erupted in Riyadh, Beirut, Cairo, Tripoli, Baghdad, Islamabad, Jakarta, Tehran, Ankara, Jericho, Khartoum, and East Jerusalem. Taxi drivers, shop owners, students, soldiers, teachers, clerics, professionals, and laborers danced in the streets, handed out candy to passersby, shouted gleefully, fired weapons in the air, and sang jubilant songs of victory.

Elisabetta Burba, an Italian journalist, was vacationing with her husband in Beirut that day. She had been at the National Museum, discovering anew the wonders of the ancient Phoenicians. That was when she first heard the news. In horrified disbelief, Burba immediately burst into tears. But as distressing as that initial shock was, far more distressing was the shock she felt as she left the museum and made her way into the city. "Walking downtown," she said, "I realized that the offspring of the great civilization I'd just seen chronicled in the museum were now celebrating a terrorist outrage. And I am not talking about destitute people. Those who were cheering belonged to the elite of the Paris of Middle East: professionals wearing double-breasted suits, charming blond ladies, pretty teenagers in tailored jeans. Trying to find our bearings, my husband and I went into an American-style café in the Hamra district, near Rue Verdun, rated as one of the most expensive shopping streets in the world. Here the cognitive dissonance was immediate, and direct. The café's sophisticated clientele was celebrating, laughing, cheering and making jokes, as waiters served hamburgers and Diet Pepsis. Nobody looked shocked, or moved. They were excited, very excited. An hour later, at a little market near the U.S. Embassy, on the outskirts of Beirut, a thrilled shop assistant showed us, using his hands, how the plane had crashed into the twin towers. He, too, was laughing."[2]

Burba and her husband quickly made their way back to their hotel, thoroughly shaken. Turning on the television, she started scanning the international channels. Again she was shocked. There were reports of Palestinians celebrating in the streets—though commentators were quick to reassure viewers that such sentiments represented only a tiny minority of the population. Later that evening, she decided to ask some moderate Arabs if that was in fact the case. "Nonsense," said one, speaking for many. "Ninety percent of the Arab world believes that the Americans got what they deserved." An exaggeration? Hyperbole? Hardly. "Perhaps," Burba concluded with no little disgust, "it is actually an understatement."

Is it possible that the Islamic world was really united in its tacit support of the terrorists? Standing in the verdant courtyard of the American Colony Hotel in East Jerusalem, Azmi Bishara, an Arab-Israeli member of parliament, explained, "There was a joyous feeling that the all-powerful America was suddenly vulnerable." According to Bishara, there was a strong sense, even among moderate Muslims, that "at last, a new balance of terror has been struck. After a decade in which America could do as it pleased anywhere in the world, from Iraq to Serbia, the poor and disenfranchised are finally rising up against her." Though Bishara said he was horrified by the sight of people jumping to their deaths from the blazing towers and he felt genuine sympathy for the victims and their families, he also felt that the "bigger picture should not be ignored. America must understand that if it turns its back on the world's poor it will get stabbed in the back. The feeling among Arabs since 1967 is that they have been under American attack."[3]

On the West Bank, a leader of the Palestinian terrorist group Hamas, Abdul al Ham'iz, spoke to a reporter by telephone. He is known for handing out candy when members of his group succeed in killing Jews. When he was asked about the celebrations that had broken out in the streets of Nablus, he said, "You don't understand. Without America, the Jews are nothing. We would have defeated the Jews a long time ago, just as the Prophet

Muhammad himself defeated the Jews." Then he said, "America is the problem that lies behind all other problems."[4]

Throughout the Western world, the reaction couldn't have been more different. Flower- and candle-strewn displays of sympathy and tribute sprang up outside the American Embassies in London, Paris, Berlin, Rome, Mexico City, Stockholm, Ottawa, Brussels, Oslo, Vienna, Copenhagen, Lima, Zurich, and Prague. Memorial services were held at Westminster Abbey, Gileskirk, Notre Dame, Cologne, Chartres, Stephansdomplatz, the Vatican, St. Vladimir's, and Santo Maria. Official mourning was proclaimed, and flags were lowered. Vigils were held. Strains of "God Bless America" were heard throughout Europe, South America, and Australia. The grief was palpable across all national, political, and ethnic lines.

The contrast between the two worlds was stark. It seemed that the East-West divide had never been more pronounced. The comprehension of that harsh reality prompted the Italian prime minister, Silvio Berlusconi, to assert that the terrorist attacks—and Islam's subsequent reaction to them—were tantamount to a "declaration of war against Western civilization" and "the whole legacy of Christendom."[5]

The news media, the filters through which Americans receive their information, are reluctant to report these things. Within a week of the terrorist attacks on Washington and New York, it had become politically incorrect to describe the Islamic militants who blew up the World Trade Center and Pentagon, murdering thousands of innocent Americans, as "Islamic" militants. The Religion Newswriters Association suggested that journalists avoid all such labeling. The organization released a statement saying that it was "troubled" by the close scrutiny given to the beliefs of Muslims in the days after the terrorist attacks in New York and Washington. So, at its annual meeting, members adopted a resolution rejecting "all phrases that might associate an entire religion with the actions of a few."

But as if that were not enough, according to David Kupelian, managing editor of *WorldNetDaily*, even the word *terrorists* was being questioned as an appropriate description of the perpetrators of the crimes. Stephen Jukes, global director of news for Reuters, decreed that the giant wire service's 2,500 journalists should not use the *T* word unless it appeared in a direct quote. "We all know that one man's terrorist is another man's freedom fighter and that Reuters upholds the principle that we do not use the word terrorist," he wrote in an internal memo. "To be frank, it adds little to call the attack on the World Trade Center a terrorist attack."[6] Attempting to explain his values-neutral approach, Jukes added, "We're trying to treat everyone on a level playing field, however tragic it's been and however awful and cataclysmic for the American people and people around the world."[7]

"Islam is a religion of peace," we are told, and the terrorists—what else are we supposed to call them really?—are just a few bad apples who belong to a widely dispersed "terror network." But as Middle East expert Daniel Pipes has asserted, we can hardly dismiss Osama bin Laden and his widespread Al Qaeda terrorist network as a "repudiated fringe form of Islamic extremism." It is hardly that. Indeed, he said, "Muslims on the streets of many places—Pakistan and Gaza in particular—are fervently rallying to the defense of Al Qaeda's vision of Islam." To call the terrorists "traitors to their own faith, trying, in effect, to hijack Islam" implies that other Muslims see them as apostates, which, he said, "is simply wrong. Al Qaeda enjoys wide popularity."[8]

So, what is the real story? Is Islam the intractable enemy of peace, freedom, and civilization the terrorists make it out to be? Or is it, as the moderates and the media would have us believe, like Christianity and Judaism: a great religion of true devotion, piety, and moral uprightness? What do Muslims really believe? What does the Koran really teach? How do we account for the seemingly contradictory character of the faith in this current crisis—and throughout its long history of conflict with the West?

The Prophet and His Faith

The compelling attraction of Islam—the fastest-growing religion in the world, already boasting nearly 1.5 billion adherents worldwide—is simple to understand. It is its simplicity. In a complex world filled with complex dilemmas, its simplicity breaks into the affairs of men and nations as a great relief. Hilaire Belloc observed, "An eclectic product of feral desert Paganism, phobic Christian heresies, and frenetic Judaism, Islam was a fierce new thing in the world. But why did this new, energetic heresy enjoy such sudden and overwhelming success? One answer is that it won battles. Another is that its doctrine was so starkly simple, which is not to say simplistic."[9]

Islam sprang up out of the desolate desert realm of the Arabian Hejaz early in the seventh century. At the age of forty, Muhammad—a wealthy merchant from the religious and commercial center of Mecca—had a series of what he took to be divine visions in a cave on the nearby Mount Hira. Because he was a charismatic leader and a member of the ruling tribe of Koreish, he quickly drew a small dedicated following of local citizens. While his fervent revelations of a sparse monotheistic faith and the promise of an afterlife captivated some, they disturbed many others, including most of the leaders of the city. Mecca owed its wealth and prosperity to its strategic location at the crossroads of several caravan routes. Its businesses catered to the traveling merchants who crossed the barren desert. It was a center for sundry entertainments of the flesh—both licit and illicit. Its great temple, the Ka'ba, was a pantheon to all the gods of East and West with shrines celebrating everything from the familiar Greek, Roman, and Persian hosts to the stern desert gods led by the Zeus-like Jinn the Arabians called Allah. It was a city of ribald excesses and confused extravagances.

Muhammad had grown up listening to the vivid stories of the rugged travelers and adventurers who enlivened Mecca. His imagination was stirred by tales of far-off places and the gods who purportedly ruled them. The chaotic diversity of the world disturbed his sense of order while it inspired his sense of purpose. He began to wander the arid hills and mountains, dreaming and plotting.

Borrowing from the desert paganism of his ancestors as well as from the hybrid faiths of the heretical Arians, Nestorians, and Zoroastrians, he cobbled together a very simple and practical vision of the world. His new faith was, he believed, actually not new at all but was, in fact, the oldest of all religions. It was, he thought, an aboriginal and natural form of monotheism. He was convinced that this newly conceived Islam was man's original and unadulterated religion from which all other religions, including Judaism and Christianity, had eventually derived through a series of corruptions and apostasies.

It all seemed so obvious to the prophet. His faith boiled down the essence of all the others to the most basic and foundational truths. Its sparse simplicity was evidence that Islam's creedless faith contained all that man needed to know and do in order to please God. Muhammad was sure that his synthesis was pure genius.

The leaders of Mecca thought that Muhammad was delusional. But worse, his ardent visions, violent preaching, and pointed denunciations were proving detrimental to business as usual. So, in 622, they sent him and his handful of recently converted disciples into exile.

The self-proclaimed prophet was forced to flee to the nearby agricultural settlement of Yathrib, which he shortly renamed Medina, where he was able to drum up more reliable support. There, he began to systematize his theological dogmas, regularize his social inclinations, and institutionalize his militant vision of politics—together comprising a comprehensive cultural pattern that he was convinced fate had already determined would ultimately sweep across the entire earth.

Eventually the prophet built his band of followers into a ruthless army. After consolidating control over the central Arabian desert, he launched a bloody assault on Mecca. Thus, in 630, the first of Islam's many revolutionary conquests was accomplished. The conquests would continue through the entire Middle East, across North Africa, into the heart of Asia, upward to the Russian steppes and even toward Europe across the Balkans and the Pyrenees. No nation has ever peacefully converted to Islam; every Islamic nation was brought under the dominion of Muhammad's sickle by Muhammad's sword.

Five Pillars

While Islam shared with Christianity and Judaism a belief in a single, sovereign, and almighty God, a heavenly afterlife, a spiritual realm populated with angels and demons, and a strict ethical code of conduct governing the whole of life, the real distinctive of his simple but all-encompassing spiritual vision was what Muhammad called the Five Pillars of submission. Although he never particularly emphasized the necessity of understanding the other aspects Islamic dogma, keeping these Islamic disciplines was absolutely essential. Anyone who kept them was a faithful *Umma,* a true believer. Anyone who did not was a *Kafir,* an infidel. Such a straightforward standard of works-righteousness made the life of faith an extraordinarily simple, quantifiable, and mechanical process.

In other words, while Islam shared a number of important doctrines and dogmas with the two other great Abrahamic faiths, its essential difference was that it taught a means of salvation attainable and achievable by human agency. Man can save himself. In Islam, there is no real comprehension of the Fall. In Christianity, men are "by nature children of wrath" (Eph. 2:3), and therefore require the redemptive work of Christ. Because men are fallen, they need to be saved by a means that they cannot manufacture or conjure themselves. Likewise, in Judaism men "have all turned aside, they have together become corrupt; there is none who does good, no, not one" (Ps. 14:3 NKJV). The doctrine of the Fall means that "Salvation is of the Lord" (Jonah 2:9). But, for a good Muslim, a keeping of the Five Pillars can actually ensure salvation. There is no need of redemption, just discipline.

The first pillar or discipline of Islam was the *Shahada,* or profession of faith. There were no complex creeds to be recited. There were no complex theological equations to be memorized. There were no complex mysteries to be resolved. The *Umma,* the good and sincere Muslim, need only recite, "There is no god but Allah and Muhammad is his prophet." It could hardly have been any simpler.

The second pillar or discipline of Islam was the *Salat,* or prayer ritual. At first performed twice a day, later three times a day, and finally codified by the prophet at five times a day, the performance of these rote petitions and prostrations was the heart of the Muslim's devotional piety. There were no arcane liturgies. There were no elaborate ceremonies. There were no intricate rites. There were no inexplicable sacraments. The height of worship was bowing toward Mecca and chanting the intercessory formula. Nothing more was required. It could hardly have been any simpler.

The third pillar or discipline of Islam was the *Zakat,* or alms levy or tax. Every good Muslim was to give to the needs of the poor, for the benefit of the community, and in support of the expansion of the faith. There was no set formula or percentage for this stewardship. There was no mandatory tithe. There was no objective standard to gauge it against. Giving was to be generous. Again, it could hardly have been any simpler.

The fourth pillar or discipline of Islam was the *Haj,* or pilgrimage. Every good Muslim was to travel, at least once in his life, to visit Mecca and to pray at the monolithic pantheon, the Ka'ba. Though there were certain rituals and traditions associated with such a trip, it was essentially designed to be a once-in-a-lifetime opportunity to walk where the prophet had walked. It could hardly have been any simpler.

The fifth pillar of Islam was the *Saum,* or fasting ritual. Once a year, during the month of Ramadan, the good Muslim is to abstain from all food and drink during the daylight hours. There were no other great festivals to keep. There was no liturgical calendar to follow. There were no seasonal adjustments to make. It could hardly have been any simpler.

Good Muslims were to obey a number of additional mandates—

abstaining from alcohol, maintaining sexual fidelity within the bounds of polygamy, yielding all fealty to authority, and observing certain dietary restrictions—but the crux of Islamic piety was concentrated in these five signs of submission to Allah. The very word *Islam* means "submission."

Martin Luther, the German Augustinian monk who launched the Reformation at the beginning of the sixteenth century often asserted that biblical religion stood on the firm foundation of the doctrine of the Fall. In fact, he said that first word of the gospel was *guilt*. Men are judicially condemned because of both their original and their volitional sin. The second word of the gospel was *want*. Men lack the means and the competency to rectify their guilty estate. Sinful is what they are not just what they do. They are therefore in need of a Redeemer, a Savior, and a Mediator. Only after these first and second words have been pronounced are men ready to hear the third word of the gospel, Luther asserted. That third word was *substitution*—the justifying, propitiating, and atoning substitutionary work of the Messiah. In Islam, because there was no conception of the Fall, there was no need for substitution. Submission was enough.

The simple faith of Muhammad was therefore merely that man was adequate. Man could make his own way, earn his own salvation, and exercise his own discipline. For all its praise of Allah, Islam has always been a man-centered faith.

The *Umma* and Infidelity

According to Muhammad, faithful and disciplined submission to Allah was ultimately to be universal. Any resistance to such submission was an unholy affront. Thus, men and nations were to be brought into submission by any means at the disposal of the *Umma*, including force, if necessary. A kind of righteous war, or *Ji'had*, might be waged on such infidelity.

The faith, being so simple and straightforward, was not likely to be misunderstood. It did not require the creeds, councils, and canons of Christianity. It did not depend upon the philosophical speculations of Judaism. It did not demand the cryptic mathematical calculations of Zoroastrianism. To Muhammad's mind, the only possible reason men or nations might resist or reject Allah's plain revelations was obstinate rebellion. Such recalcitrance had to be dealt with harshly, lest it spread its complex perversions far and wide. Infidelity had to be destroyed.

Muhammad was unambiguous on this matter. The Koran made this abundantly clear:

When Ramadan is over, slay the idolaters wherever you find them. Arrest them, besiege them, and lie in ambush everywhere for them. If they repent and take to prayer and render the alms levy, allow them to go their way. Allah is forgiving and merciful. (9:5)

Strike terror into the hearts of the enemies of God, who are also your enemies. (8:60)

Kill the infidels, and God will torment them and cover them with shame. (9:14)

The punishment of those who wage war against Allah and his Prophet and strive to make mischief in the land is only this, that they should be murdered or crucified or their hands and their feet should be cut off on opposite sides or they should be imprisoned;

this shall be as a disgrace for them in this world, and in the here-
after they shall have a grievous chastisement. (5:33)

I will instill terror into the hearts of the infidels, smite them above
their necks and smite all their finger-tips off them. It is not you
who slay them; it is Allah. (8:13; 17)

Umma, take neither Jews nor Christians for your friends. They
are friends with one another. Whoever of you seeks their friendship will become one of their number. Allah does not guide such
infidels. (5:51)

Prophet, make war on the infidels and the hypocrites and deal
rigorously with them. Hell shall be their home: an evil fate. (9:73)

Fight against such of those to whom the Scriptures were given as
believe neither in Allah nor the Last Day, who do not forbid what
Allah and his prophet have forbidden and do not embrace the
true faith until they pay tribute out of hand and are utterly subdued. (9:26)

Muhammad is Allah's prophet. Those who follow him are ruthless to the infidels but merciful to one another. (48:29)

Let those who would exchange the life of this world for the here-
after, fight for the cause of Allah; whether they die or conquer. We
shall richly reward them. (4:74)

Do not say that those who were slain in the cause of Allah are
dead; they are alive, although you are not aware of them. (2:151)

Fight for the sake of Allah those that fight against you, but do not attack them first. Allah does not love the aggressors. Kill them wherever you find them. Drive them out of the places from which they drove you. Idolatry is worse than carnage. But do not fight them within the precincts of the Holy Mosque unless they attack you there. (2:190)

Umma, why is it that when it is said to you "March in the cause of Allah" you linger slothfully in the land? Are you content with that life in preference to the life of Paradise? Few indeed are the blessings of this life, compared to those of the life to come. (9:38)

Whether unarmed or well equipped, march on and fight for the cause of Allah with your wealth and your persons. (9:41)

You, the *Umma,* are the best of peoples, evolved for mankind. All others are inferior. (3:110)

Those who believe fight in the way of Allah and those who disbelieve fight in the way of the Satan. (4:76)

Surely Allah loves those who fight in his way in ranks as if they were a firm and compact wall. He it is who sent his prophet with the guidance and the true religion, that he may make it overcome the religions, all of them, though the infidel Christians may be averse. O you who believe! Shall I lead you to a merchandise which may deliver you from a painful chastisement? You shall believe in Allah and his prophet, and struggle hard in Allah's way with your property and your lives; that is better for you, did you but know! He will forgive you your faults and cause you to enter into gardens, beneath which rivers flow, and goodly dwellings in gardens of perpetuity; that is the mighty achievement and good news to the *Umma*. (61:4, 9–13)

If any one desires a religion other than Islam, never will it be accepted of him. (3:85)

Fight them on, until there is no more tumult, seduction, or oppression, and there prevail justice, faith in Allah, and the religion becomes Islam. (2:193)

If you are slain, or die in the way of Allah, forgiveness and mercy from Allah are far better than all they could amass. (3:157)

Fight those who do not believe in Allah, nor in the latter day, nor do they prohibit what Allah and his prophet have prohibited, nor follow the religion of truth of the people of the Book, (re: Jews and the Christians) until they pay the Jizya (the tax imposed upon them) with willing submission and feel themselves subdued. (9:29)

The Hadith was an early anthology of the sayings, legends, and parables of Muhammad, and it is the second most important sacred text in the Islamic faith. Compiled by the prophet's successors, the caliphs, it, too, was unambiguous about the posture of the *Umma* to infidels who had the audacity to disdain such simple truths and such obvious virtues:

Wherever you find the infidels, kill them, for whoever kills them shall have reward on the Day of Resurrection. (9:4)

I have been ordered by God to fight with people till they bear testimony to the fact that there is no God but Allah and that Muhammad is his messenger, and that they establish prayer and pay Zakat. If they do it, their blood and their property are safe from me. (1:13)

Muhammad said, "I have been ordered to fight with the people till they say, none has the right to be worshipped but Allah." (4:196)

Muhammad also said, "Know that paradise is under the shade of the swords." (4:73)

Muhammad said, "Whoever changes his Islamic religion, kill him." (9:57)

Muhammad said: "No *Umma* should be killed for killing a *Kafir*." (9:50)

Muhammad once was asked: "What is the best deed for the Muslim next to believing in Allah and his Prophet?" His answer was, "To participate in *Ji'had*, in Allah's cause." (1:25)

Muhammad also said, "The person who participates in *Ji'had* and nothing compels him to do so except belief in Allah and his prophet, will be recompensed by Allah either with a reward, or booty, or he will be admitted to paradise." (1:35)

One justification offered by Islam's modern advocates for this irrefutable militancy is that such passages are often snatched out of their cultural and historical context. Karen Armstrong is a former Catholic nun who has written widely to assert the essential peacefulness of the Muslim faith. She has published a popular history of Islam, a biography of Muhammad, and a chronicle of the Crusades. Writing in *Time* magazine in the days immediately following the terrorist attacks on New York and Washington, she stated, "Because the Koran was revealed in the context of an all-out war, several passages deal with the conduct of armed struggle. Warfare was a desperate business on the Arabian Peninsula. A chieftain was not expected to spare survivors after a battle, and some of the Koranic injunctions seem to share this spirit."[10]

The difficulty with such an apology is that it is fraught with false assumptions. Muhammad was not at war with anyone when he began dictating the Suras of the Koran. Rather, he was a prosperous citizen of a leading family in a peaceful commercial center, which had not known armed conflict for many years. War came only after he revealed his plans to cleanse Mecca of its *Kafir*, its infidels. In addition, when the Koranic visions were revealed, Muhammad was not a chieftain either. He spent most of his days wandering and dreaming in the mountains. And in any case, he did not share in the spirit of the other chieftains, which is precisely why they chose to rid themselves of the nuisance he had created in their midst by sending him into exile.

Islam, as it was conceived by the prophet, was from beginning to end a violent, intolerant, and militant faith. Not surprisingly Islam has wreaked havoc on the civilizations it has come into contact with, beginning with Byzantium in the seventh century and continuing to the present with the United States and the Western alliance.

Terrorism has virtually always been a part of its strategy for dealing with infidel nations. Early on, the Muslims launched what they called *Aza'sin*, or forceful cleansing. Armed mobs would sweep aside native populations with looting, pillaging, and genocidal triage. Some of the most zealous young men were set aside as *Fidah'is*, or suicide assassins. Later, the Ottoman Turks utilized the terror tactics of the *Assassini*, or assassins, to bring whole nations under subjection. And still later, they created the *Janissaries*, a corps of conscripted terrorists.

Islam was creedless, but it was not heedless. Its stark simplicity lent it a mad certainty about its mission to simply cleanse the world of its complex recalcitrance.

A Faithful Son

Osama bin Laden, the son of a multibillionaire Saudi construction magnate, was born in 1957, the seventeenth of fifty-three children. He was raised in a very strict and pious Islamic home where he received careful theological training. He became a Koranic scholar and took every word of the sacred text very seriously.

It is hardly surprising then that he was an early supporter of the *Mujaheddin* resistance movement formed to oppose the Soviet invasion of Afghanistan in 1979 with a fierce *Ji'had*. "I was enraged," he has said. "So, I went there at once." At first, his role was limited to fund-raising activities in Pakistan. Toward the end of the war, however, he moved to Afghanistan and took part in several battles against the Soviet army.

At the time, the Afghan *Mujaheddin* were receiving financial and logistical support from the United States and other Western governments. Osama saw little difference between the United States and the Soviet Union, however. In his view, both superpowers were equally culpable—both were manifestations of infidel nations imposing infidel values on the Islamic world.

According to former associates of Osama, his anger at the United States grew after the Persian Gulf War in 1991. He was particularly scandalized by the decision to station thousands of troops in Saudi Arabia. In a lengthy statement in 1996 outlining his philosophy, he denounced the "occupation" of the Arab holy lands by "American Crusader forces," which he described as "the latest and greatest aggression" against the Islamic world since the death of the prophet Muhammad in 632.

Because of his strident opposition to the Saudi alliance with the United States, Osama was placed under house arrest in Jiddah, Saudi Arabia. But then in April 1991, he fled the country, moving first to Afghanistan and then to the Sudanese capital, Khartoum. A fundamentalist Islamic government had just come to power in Sudan and was permitting Muslims to enter the country without visas, opening the doors for hundreds of suspected terrorists and former *Mujaheddin*. Osama used his stay in Sudan to set up legitimate businesses and to prepare for a terrorist war against the United States.

Eventually Sudan expelled Osama and most of his supporters after the United States mounted political and diplomatic pressure. He decided to move back to Afghanistan, which had recently fallen into the hands of a revolutionary band of former theology students known as the Taliban. Under the sponsorship of this rogue government of terror, Osama began using his vast wealth to set up training camps in the mountains. According to Ahmed Ressam, an Algerian terrorist operative trained by bin Laden who was arrested on the Canadian border in December 1999, the camps offered training in such wide-ranging skills as bomb making, rocket launching, urban warfare, assassination, and sabotage.

The network of terror that Osama built through his training camps included citizens from dozens of countries, including Saudi Arabia, Algeria, Jordan, Pakistan, Libya, Egypt, Indonesia, Malaysia, and the United States, and boast operations, both legal and illegal, in some forty nations around the globe.

In a 1999 *Time* magazine interview Osama ably justified his tactics by appealing to the Koran, to Islamic tradition, and to the history of the struggle of Islam against Western civilization. He portrayed himself as a new Saladin called forth by Allah to resist yet another wave of crusading infidels.[11] In other words, he claimed that he was standing foursquare in the center of Islamic orthodoxy. He was a simple man who simply believed his simple faith. His militancy was but a measured response to the blind obstinacy of the *Kafir* Jews and their American sponsors. His violence and intolerance were but faithful responses to Islam's threatened purity.

The Koran

Does that mean that all good Muslims are likewise inclined to be violent, intolerant, and militant? Are the so-called Muslim moderates just being disingenuous and dishonest? Are they kidding us—or even kidding themselves—when they publicly distance themselves from Osama and his terrorist cabal? No, not at all. The fact is, the vast majority of all Muslims—like so many Christians and Jews—do not know what their faith actually teaches beyond the bare essentials.

The revelation of Islam came to Muhammad over the course

of a decade, between 610 and 620, in a series of 114 visions. The prophet dictated these Suras to his disciples, who recorded them as the Koran. These episodic units varied widely in length, subject, style, and coherence. But together, they comprised the basis of all Islamic beliefs.

Alas, the Koran was written in classic Arabic and was, by the prophet's decree, not to be translated, lest the accretions of error slip back into this one, true, original religion. That decree has meant that most Muslims have never been able to read the sacred writings of their religion for themselves. Islam has developed more as a series of spiritual disciplines—essentially the Five Pillars and their handful of ancillary duties—than as a coherent set of spiritual doctrines. It relies more on an orthopraxy than an orthodoxy. What a Muslim does is a far more important measure of his faith than what he knows. A good Muslim might be quite ignorant of some of the most basic teachings of the Koran. As long as he holds to the essential patterns of life and faith, he remains an *Umma*.

Most moderate Muslims would be horrified to discover that Osama bin Laden may represent their faith more honestly, more literally, and more faithfully than they do. Those Muslims, and particularly those American Muslims, who have decried the terrorist tactics of Osama, the tyranny of the Taliban in Afghanistan, the crass cruelty of the Palestinian *Intifada,* the brazen defiance of Saddam in Iraq, or the angry ravings of the Mullahs in Iran, have been spared the difficulty of consistency by their ignorance. That combined with the fact that liberal, modernist, and moderate Muslims often do not literally interpret the mandates of Islam means that most hard-working, peace-loving Muslims really are just hard-working, peace-loving neighbors.

That glorious inconsistency affords Christians in the West a tremendous opportunity. The conflict between what many Muslims actually believe and what they are supposed to believe creates a worldview crisis that may well give us a chance to reach a whole new generation with the good news of the gospel.

In today's post–terrorist-attack world where the existence of evil is now difficult to deny, where the sinfulness of man is difficult to ignore, and where the reality of the Fall is difficult to avoid, the chance to get to the first and second words of the gospel in conversations with our Muslim neighbors has never been easier or more opportune. Indeed, this clash of worldviews may well turn out to be the most beneficent result of these dire and difficult days.

Worldviews

When the subject of worldview comes up, we generally think of the intricacies of philosophy. We think of intellectual niggling. We think of the brief and blinding oblivion of ivory tower speculation, of thickly obscure tomes, and of inscrutable logical complexities.

But a worldview is as practical as potatoes. It is far less metaphysical than understanding marginal market buying at the stock exchange or legislative initiatives in Congress. It is far less esoteric than typing a book into a laptop computer or sending a fax across the continent.

The word itself is a poor English attempt at translating the German *weltanschauung*. It literally means a "life perspective" or "a way of seeing."[12] It is the way we look at the world.

You have a worldview. I have a worldview. Osama bin Laden has a worldview. Everyone does. It is our perspective. It is our frame of reference. It is the means by which we interpret the situations and circumstances around us. It enables us to integrate all the different aspects of our faith, life, and experience.

In his book *Future Shock* Alvin Toffler wrote, "Every person carries in his head a mental model of the world, a subjective representation of external reality."[13] This mental model is, he argued, like a giant filing cabinet. It contains a slot for every item of information coming to us. It organizes our knowledge and gives us a grid from which to think. The mind is not as Pelagius, Locke, Voltaire, or Rousseau would have had us suppose—a *tabula rasa,* a blank slate. No one is completely open-minded or genuinely objective. "When we think," said economic philosopher E. F. Schumacher, "we can only do so because our mind is already filled with all sorts of ideas with which to think."[14] These more or less fixed notions make up our mental model of the world, our frame of reference, our presuppositions—in other words, our worldview.

James Sire has written:

> A worldview is a map of reality; and like any map, it may fit what is actually there, or it may be grossly misleading. The map is not the world itself of course, only an image of it, more or less accurate in some places, distorted in others. Still, all of us carry around such a map in our mental makeup and we act upon it. All our thinking presupposes it. Most of our experience fits into it.[15]

A worldview is simply a way of viewing the world.

The Christian worldview, with its appreciation for the potentialities and the liabilities of this poor fallen world, has spawned a remarkable flowering of freedom, prosperity, and tolerance. The

Islamic worldview, with its emphasis on discipline and conquest, has spawned little more than poverty, tyranny, and terror.

The primary difference between a genuinely integrated Christian worldview and any other religious system is that in Christianity men are called to despair of their own competency while other religions call men to rise to a new level of spiritual prowess by their own efforts or disciplines. The former is an exercise in repentance while the latter is a kind of works-righteousness. The first depends on the work of God's grace; the other depends on the submission of man's ambitions.

The message of the gospel is that "God so loved the world, that He gave His only begotten Son" (John 3:16). Though the world is "in the power of the evil one" (1 John 5:19), God is "in Christ reconciling the world to Himself" (2 Cor. 5:19). Jesus is the "Light of the world" (John 8:12). He is the "Savior of the world" (John 4:42). He is the "Lamb of God who takes away the sin of the world" (John 1:29). He was made "the propitiation for our sins; and not for ours only, but also for those of the whole world" (1 John 2:2). Through Christ, all things are reconciled to the Father (Col. 1:20) so that finally the kingdoms of this world shall become the "kingdom of our Lord, and of His Christ" (Rev. 11:15).

The message of Islam is that man is capable of yielding himself to a higher calling, a higher way, and a higher purpose by sheer volition and discipline. And therein lies all the difference.

Throughout the ages, men like Cain have used their man-centered religions to get what they want.[16] Men like Balaam have used their man-centered religions to control circumstances.[17] Men like Korah have used their man-centered religions to enhance their position.[18] Cain, Balaam, and Korah all believed in the universal power of imposed law. They believed that not only could they

58

manipulate human society and natural elements with some sort of legal system, but that God would be forced to conform Himself to the desires and demands of men who act in terms of their notion of law: say certain things, do certain things, believe certain things, or act out certain things, and God will have to respond. In essence, they believed that man controlled his own destiny, using rituals and formulas of law like magic to save mankind, to shape history, to govern society, and to manipulate God.

The great lesson of human history is that men are forever rejecting the grace of God, going "the way of Cain," rushing "headlong into the error of Balaam," and perishing "in the rebellion of Korah" (Jude 11). That is the reason why tyrannical statism has always been so predominant among rebellious men and nations. For if law can somehow save mankind, shape history, govern society, and manipulate God, then obviously men must work to institute a total law-order. If the rituals and formulas of law are indeed like magic, then men must erect a comprehensive state to govern men comprehensively. Communism was that kind of saving law-order. It attempted to rule every aspect of life and to solve every dilemma of life through the agency of the omnipotent, omnipresent state. Similarly Islam is a saving law-order. It attempts to create a theocratic paradise based upon the coercive enforcement of the simple mandates of the Koran. It attempts to create a top-down government, manufacturing salvation by mechanical submission.

In the end, such a worldview necessarily collapses under the weight of its own absurdity. And that may very well provide the evangelistic bridge to the Muslim community that Christians have been seeking for generations. As Muslims are confronted by the gross differences between what they actually believe and what they are supposed to believe, opportunities for witness, service, outreach, friendship, hospitality, mercy, kindness, forbearance, love, and even conversion will naturally abound.

For far too long Christians have treated Muslims as our ideological adversaries. We have seen them as our enemies. To be sure, theirs is a worldview that by its very nature is an affront to Western civilization, a threat to our liberties, and an attack on our values—but then so is every other form of unbelief. The biblical mandate for Christians is not to argue with, shun, or stigmatize unbelief, but to win it.

When the wars are over, when justice has been secured, when the revolutionary cells have been rooted out, and when the physical threats of terror have been contained, then it is time for Christians to cross the bridge built by the two faces of Islam for the sake of the Great Commission.

The Great Commission

"The earth is the LORD's" (Ps. 24:1). God has not limited the jurisdiction of His sovereignty to heaven. Despite the disruption of the Fall, He continues to execute His authority over the world with "an everlasting kingdom" (Dan. 4:3). He rules it from His throne on high (Ps. 11:4). That is clear enough. At the same time, though, He graciously apportions it out to His people. He commissions us to exercise stewardship over it. We are to be more than just salt: preserving. We are to be light: reclaiming (Matt. 5:13–16). Justice, mercy, and humility before God are to be tandem virtues in our lives as we reach out to a lost and dying world.

This is the crux of a balanced biblical worldview. And it is dramatically underscored in Christ's final instructions to His disciples in the Great Commission. He said, "All authority has been given to Me in heaven and on earth. Go therefore and make disciples of all the nations, baptizing them in the name of the Father and the Son and the Holy Spirit, teaching them to observe all that I commanded you; and lo, I am with you always, even to the end of the age" (Matt. 28:18–20).

All authority in heaven is His, of course. The heights and the depths, the angels and the principalities are all under His sovereign rule. But all authority on earth is His as well. Man and creature, as well as every invention and institution, are under His sovereign rule. There are no neutral areas in all of the cosmos that escape the authority of the Lord Jesus Christ (Col. 1:17).

Therefore, on this basis, the Commission states that believers are to extend Christ's kingdom, making disciples by going, baptizing, and teaching—wherever unbelief may be found in all the nations of the earth. This mandate is the essence of the new covenant, which is an extension of the old covenant: go and begin the process of reclaiming everything in heaven and on earth for His name's sake (Gen. 1:28). We are called to be a part of what will, in the fullness of time, "bring all things in heaven and on earth together under one head, even Christ" (Eph. 1:10 NIV).

The emphasis is inescapable: we are not to stop with simply telling the fallen men and nations that Jesus is Lord; we are to demonstrate His lordship in our families, in our churches, in our work, in our communities, and in our culture. We are to make disciples who will obey everything that He has commanded, not just in a hazy zone of piety, but in the totality of life by demonstrating the very principles of redemptive grace and mercy that we proclaim.

This is the thrust of the Great Commission. It is the spiritual, emotional, and cultural mandate to win the fallen world for Jesus. And though we know that only Christ Himself can fulfill that mandate in its entirety at the close of human history, our duty is to trust and obey, work and pray, love and serve, minister and administer. We are to "occupy till [He comes]" (Luke 19:13 KJV).

A biblical worldview necessarily embraces the comprehensive implications of the Great Commission—in word and in deed, in going and proclaiming, in standing for gospel mercy and standing for substitutionary justice in this fallen world. It applies Scripture to every area of life and godliness. The fact is, the salvation of fallen souls is the immediate aim of the Great Commission. But the more ultimate aim is the promotion of the glory of the triune God (Rom. 16:25–27). We must have a passion for souls (2 Cor. 5:11). We must take every opportunity (Col. 4:5), expend every energy (2 Cor. 6:4–10), and risk every expense (Acts 4:29) beseeching men to be reconciled to God (2 Cor. 5:20). But individualistic redemption is not the be-all and end-all of the Great Commission.

The Fall affected both men and nations, both souls and societies, and both individuals and institutions. The Fall is comprehensive so the presentation of the gospel must be comprehensive. Our evangelism must include sociology as well as salvation; it must include a new social order as well as a new birth; it must include reform and redemption, culture and conversion, a reformation and a regeneration. Read the sermons of the great evangelists through the ages and you will immediately see that kind of balance—they invariably begin by addressing the grave injustices of the day, proceed to tender examples of human need, and conclude with a vital appeal to reconcile with Christ. They move from the first word of the gospel, to the second, and finally to the third. Regardless of the text, the outline is simple: guilt, want, and substitution in need of justice, mercy, and humility before God.

Any other kind of evangelism is shortsighted and woefully impotent, which may be why so many of the efforts to reach the Muslim community have failed so miserably in the past. Any other kind of evangelism fails to live up to the comprehensive high call of the Great Commission and the very essence of the gospel. We can and we must reach out to the adherents of this simple faith with the glorious truth.

Chapter Four

The Sons of Ham

Love, friendship, and respect do not unite people as much as a
common hatred for something.

—ANTON CHEKHOV

All of Iraq's most prominent Islamic leaders representing virtually every variant branch of that stern eclectic faith—from the
Sunnis to the Shi'ites, from the Zaydis to the Ismailis, from the
Sufis to Wahhabis, from the Marabouts to the Senussi, and from
the Druze to the Alawites—were present at the lavish pagan festival. But there were no cries of outrage, no sworn condemna-
tions, no angry anathemas, and no holy *fatwahs.* The entire event
was taken very much in stride. It was, after all, a day of national
pride—a rare opportunity for them to come together acknowl-
edging their common roots. They conferred on it their whole-
hearted *Ijma,* their unanimous approval.

It was the festival of the ancient Mesopotamian goddess of fertility, Ishtar. Celebrated in a newly consecrated temple district, it
was to be the centerpiece of Saddam Hussein's week-long revelry.
It commemorated the end of his bloody, costly conflict with Iran
in 1989.

The bronze talisman of Ishtar, a faithful reproduction of an ancient idol from the time of Nebuchadnezzar, was unveiled. Incense bathed the entire vicinity with an air of sanctity. Ethereal music lilted in the breeze. Costumed attendants bearing torches led a long processional in a triumphant march. Then, as if this were the moment they had all been waiting for, Saddam Hussein stepped onto a strobe-lit platform and announced the commencement of a new world order, taking the ancient pledge of kings: "I will wash my hands and my feet in the blood of the infidels for the glory of Mesopotamia forever."

The solemn clerics were pleased. The *Ji'had* had begun. The world would once again feel *Dar al Harb*—the scourge of war. Babylon was reborn.

Babylon

Sometime shortly after his debacle at Babel around 2250 B.C., Nimrod established several villages and trading centers all along the Euphrates River, including the city of Babylon. According to the Bible, Nimrod was a mighty and fearsome man who made those cultures in his own image (Gen. 10:8–12). Thus, from its earliest days Babylon and its neighbors were known for their fierceness and aggression.

A long line of strong leaders enabled Babylon to gain preeminence over all the other settlements, building the city into an imperial power with dominions ultimately stretching from the Caspian to the Nile. Though the land surrounding it was always parched and poor, Babylon used its military might to accumulate unfathomable riches. Its markets overflowed with the wealth and splendor of a thousand realms. Its profusion of magnificent architectural marvels—from the beautiful double-wide

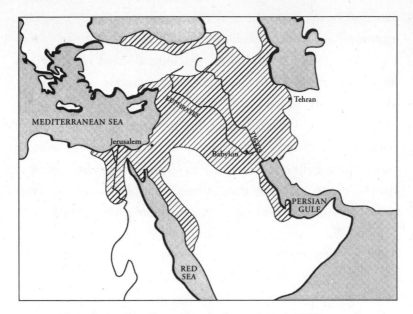

The Babylonian Empire, circa 550 B.C.

walls and crenulated towers to the broad processional avenues and multitiered temples—made it the envy of the world. Its fabled gates both awed and terrified adversaries. Its gardens, canals, and palaces dazzled visitors. Its art, literature, music, and religion set the standard for every other civilization in the ancient world. Though it suffered an occasional military humiliation or political setback at the hands of the Hittites, the Medes, the Persians, the Greeks, or even rival Mesopotamian settlements, Babylon remained the cultural and economic center of gravity in the region for nearly two millennia.

Both at home and abroad, the cruelly imposed Babylonian culture was perverse and depraved. Throughout the Bible, it epitomizes the essence of evil. Accordingly the city is variously called the furious "oppressor" (Isa. 14:4), the "everlasting desolation"

(Jer. 25:12), the "horror among the nations" (Jer. 50:23), the devastator yet to be "devastated" (Ps. 137:8), and the "mother of harlots" (Rev. 17:5). It symbolizes the fountainhead of mankind's immorality, the wellspring of earth's abominations, and the object of God's wrath (Rev. 14:8; 17:5; 16:19).

In 597 B.C., Nebuchadnezzar, the mightiest of the Babylonian kings and the renowned conqueror of the known world, swept his puissant armies into Jerusalem. With cruel efficiency he confirmed Babylon's merciless reputation. After a short but brutally debilitating siege, he captured the royal family of Jehoiachin, the high priest Seraiah, and all of the most distinguished citizens of the land. Many were forced to witness the execution of their children. The rest were dragged off into captivity in Babylon. The royal treasury was looted. The temple was ransacked and its treasures added to Nebuchadnezzar's booty. And as a final indignity, many of the survivors were driven penniless from their homes into foreign exile.

Eleven years later, in 586 B.C., Nebuchadnezzar again scourged Jerusalem. The puppet provincial government he had installed under Zedekiah had shown signs of unrest, so the Babylonian monarch determined to put an end to the Jews once and for all. A massacre followed. Rapine and destruction were unrestrained. The temple was destroyed. The royal palace and the city were set ablaze and the last of the bedraggled inhabitants deported. The prophets Ezekiel and Jeremiah recorded the awful event with grievous clarity. The true spirit and character of imperial Babylon had been disclosed.

After Nebuchadnezzar, the city began a precipitous decline and was finally destroyed and depopulated, in fulfillment of innumerable prophecies in Scripture. But the spirit of Babylon was not forgotten. In fact, the dream of reviving Babylonian glory has haunted

Mesopotamia, the region we now call Iraq, ever since. In modern times, that yearning propelled Nebuchadnezzar's progeny into one insane war after another. After the moderate young Hashemite King Faisal was assassinated in 1958, Iraqi leaders carefully followed the old empire's primeval prescription for conquest: attacking their ancient foe Israel in 1967 and 1973, invading the Kuwaiti heirs of their Mesopotamian rivals Sumer and Akkad in 1961, 1973, and 1990, and engaging their primordial Persian enemies in Iran in a devastating, protracted war from 1980 to 1988.

Early in his tenure, Saddam Hussein announced his intentions to restore Iraq's Babylonian heritage. He launched a meticulous, multi-billion-dollar excavation and reconstruction of the ancient city located sixty miles south of Baghdad, rebuilding a number of its most significant sites. They included Nebuchadnezzar's opulent grand palace, the vast Esagila temple precinct, the beautiful Via Sacra processional boulevard, and the resplendent hanging gardens of the Lugalgirra District. In addition, he rewrote the Iraqi constitution to mirror that of Hammurabi. He reformed the bureaucracy to emulate that of Merodachbaladan. He restructured the military to mimic that of Nabopolassar. He even revived academic and experimental interests in the cult of Ishtar, Babylon's ancient fertility religion that combined many of the elements of what we today call the New Age movement with various ancient pagan rituals.

Hussein fully embraced the spirit of Babylon with an unapologetic, messianic fervor. At the dedication of the newly reconstructed Ishtar Gate he said,

Glorious in a glorious time, Babylon is the lady of reviving centuries, rising dignified and holy, showing the great history of Iraq.

Added to its magnificence and emphasizing its originality, the phoenix of the new time rises alive from the ashes of the past to face the bright present—thus placing it on a golden throne, bringing back its charm, its charming youth, and unique glory. Babylon is not a city made of rocks and bricks—full of mere human events. It is not a forgotten place of the ancient past. Babylon is something else altogether. Since its birth, Babylon has stretched out its arms to the future—to be the seat of eternal wisdom, to represent the first civilization, and to remain as the glittering lighthouse in the dark night of history. Here is Babylon.[1]

The implications of these Babylonian ambitions were made plain in an official Iraqi publication, which asserted that "Saddam Hussein has emerged from Mesopotamia as did Hammurabi, as did Merodachbaladan, and as did Nebuchadnezzar. He has emerged at a time to shake the centuries-old dust off Babylon's face. History must start with us so that Babylon can remain mankind's compass throughout the ages. Spirit arise."[2]

The spirit of Babylon is not the only shade being conjured from the distant past in the Middle East. Throughout the region, the legacy of ancient glory is proving to be an irresistible catalyst for nationalistic fervor.

Assyria

At the northern end of the valley between the Tigris and Euphrates Rivers, the city of Nineveh, like Babylon, was established by Nimrod sometime after the dispersion at Babel. Although it quickly became an important commercial center, it failed to build a lasting empire of any sort for more than fifteen hundred years.

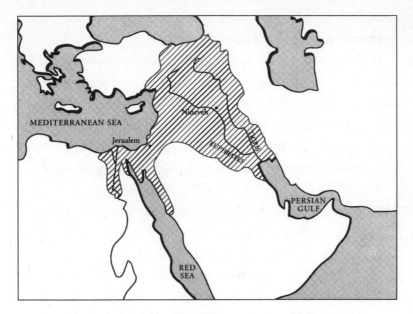

The Assyrian Empire, circa 700 B.C.

Throughout those years, the city-state was generally dominated politically and militarily by Babylon; but somehow it still
maintained its own cultural identity. And because it lay along
the primary trade routes, north to the Caspian and west to the
Mediterranean, it developed an independent source of income.
Over time, Nineveh became a huge metropolis with more than
120,000 residents. Though its architecture tended to be drab
and utilitarian, it was impressive by its sheer bulk. Its gargan-
tuan walls, for instance, were wide enough for chariots to race
twelve abreast along the top. Its homes were fairly nondescript
but commodious and well designed for extended family life. It
did produce a large body of literature and an array of creative
arts, but most of the efforts seemed to be devoted to commercial or bureaucratic themes. Even its paganism was rather sedate

compared to it raucous neighbors. Nineveh was, in short, a quiet and stable community.

By 800 B.C. it seemed poised to finally emerge from the shadow of its more flamboyant southern neighbor, Babylon. That was about the time, the Bible records, that the prophet Jonah made his reluctant visit to Nineveh. After traversing the length of the city for three days fiercely preaching the judgment of God and repentance from wickedness, he met with unprecedented success:

> The people of Nineveh believed God, proclaimed a fast, and put on sackcloth, from the greatest to the least of them. Then word came to the king of Nineveh; and he arose from his throne and laid aside his robe, covered himself with sackcloth and sat in ashes. And he caused it to be proclaimed and published throughout Nineveh by the decree of the king and his nobles, saying: "Let neither man nor beast, herd nor flock, taste anything; do not let them eat, or drink water. But let man and beast be covered with sackcloth, and cry mightily to God; yes, let every one turn from his evil way and from the violence that is in his hands. Who can tell if God will turn and relent, and turn away from His fierce anger, so that we may not perish?" (Jonah 3:5–9 NKJV)

Following this dramatic conversion of all the Assyrian people—from the highest to the lowest, including their young king, Adadnirari—God indeed relented and spared the city. And it would never be the same again.

According to the Bible, conversion is not simply an ethical or philosophical revision. It is a transformation of the very soul. It affects every detail of life. A converted individual is altogether different from what he was before. He has new motivations, new standards, and new objectives. He has a new outlook, a new way of thinking, and a new way of living. He is born anew (2 Cor. 5:17).

In the same way, when a culture is converted, it is transformed. The old disappears. The new is ushered in. Covenantal faithfulness and obedience replace covenantal rebellion and insubordination. Integrity, diligence, and productivity supplant corruption, deceit, and sloth. God's blessing covers the curse of sin (Deut. 28:1–14).

That being the case, it is not surprising to see dramatic changes in the nature of Assyrian society. Apparently several of the kings that immediately succeeded Adadnirari—notably Asshurdan, and Asshurnirari—followed his example and walked in obedience to the Lord. They entered into a warm relationship with the kingdoms of Israel and Judah (2 Kings 12–15; 2 Chron. 24–28), and tremendous wealth and power flowed into the city. In a very short period of time, Assyria dominated the entire region.

Suddenly, like a bolt out of the blue, Assyrian civilization began to flower. Economic, political, and military prowess was matched with artistic, literary, and architectural splendor. The desert bloomed as better agricultural methods were applied. Breakthrough innovations spawned new marvels of engineering. Peace and prosperity prevailed.

This blessed state was short-lived, however. Pride gave way to apostasy. Tiglath-Pileser attempted to synthesize the old paganism with faith in Jehovah. Driven more by political ambition than by theological heterodoxy, he wanted to consolidate his control on his growing empire. So long as the temple in Jerusalem remained a revival focus of affection and loyalty in the hearts and minds of his people, his security was undermined. So he diverted the locus of worship to Nineveh and the old cultus.

By the time of Shalmaneser's dynasty, the wealth and power that God had graciously bestowed on Assyria had been harnessed for wickedness. Tiglath-Pileser's polyglot theology had wrought a bitter harvest. Tyranny, brutality, and aggression were unleashed on the subjected lands of the empire. In 722 B.C., the kingdom of Israel was overrun and its people dispossessed. Later, under Sennacherib, even Jerusalem was besieged. Throughout that time, the Assyrians demonstrated their familiarity with the biblical covenant but continued their refusal to submit to it (Isa. 36:10–20).

What Tiglath-Pileser, Shalmaneser, and Sennacherib failed to recognize is that with covenantal blessings come covenantal responsibilities (Deut. 28:15–68). To whom much is given, much is required (Luke 12:48). God disciplines His prodigals, even to the point of destruction (Ezek. 31:3–16; Heb. 12:5–6). God first warned the people of Assyria and then judged them (Nah. 1:1–15; 3:12–19). While other empires rose and fell slowly over time, Assyria's course was like that of a spectacular spent rocket.

Assyria's sudden power and influence still hold a mythic sway over the people of the region, particularly in Syria, which regards itself as the heir to Nineveh's legacy. Just as the leaders of Iraq have appealed to the lure and lore of Nebuchadnezzar to spark nationalistic pride over the years, the Syrians have focused on Sennacherib and Shalmaneser.

Despite the fact that the ruins of Nineveh actually lay outside the boundaries of Syria, the Assad rulers of the realm—Hafez al Assad ruled the nation until he was recently succeeded by his son, Bashar al Assad—continually invoke the memory of Assyria's glory. In 1978, for example, on the 2,750th anniversary of the destruction of Israel, Hafez feted his close-knit Alawite community with a lavish celebration that lasted a full week. No expense was spared. The richest foods, the most exotic entertainments, and the most earthly pleasures were provided without end. The days were spent in revelry, the nights in debauchery. Speech making and ribald braggadocio punctuated the hours. Finally a solid gold statue of the ancient Assyrian deity, Ashur, was ritually dedicated with Islamic *Shahadas* and *Rakatins*.

At the height of the celebration, Hafez summarized his Assyrian ambitions for the future:

We are the heirs of Sennacherib and Shalmaneser—the greatest heroes of our nation. We have inherited their glory. We have inherited their wisdom. We have inherited their valor. But most of all, we have inherited their cause. Assyria must once again unite the Arab world against the imperialism of the Infidel, the interloping of the West, and the encroachment of the Jew.[3]

He concluded the grand event by saying,

Assyria must arise and conquer. Nothing must be able to stand in our path. Indeed nothing can stand in our path. The world is once again divided between *Dar al Islam*—the abode of faith—and *Dar al Harb*—the abode of war. Like Sennacherib, we shall sweep aside every obstacle. Like him, we shall prevail. *Ji'had. Insh'allah.*[4]

Persia

In 539 B.C. an alliance of Medes and Persians—the Mongol and Parthavian peoples of Kurdistan and the Farsi and Elamite peoples of Iran—swept across the Middle East, conquering both Babylonia and Assyria. After two thousand years of uninterrupted

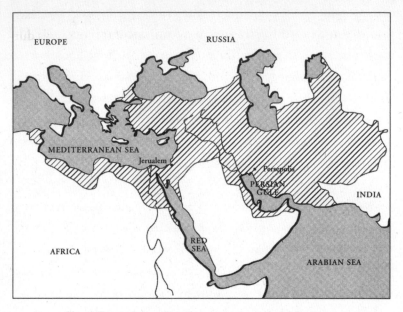

The Persian Empire, circa 400 B.C.

Arab rule, the Middle East had fallen into the hands of alien conquerors, perfectly fulfilling the prophecies of Isaiah, Jeremiah, Ezekiel, Daniel, Habakkuk, and Nahum.

The Persian rulers, from Cyrus to Xerxes and Darius to Artaxerxes, were refined and benevolent. Their culture was extravagant and cosmopolitan, and they reveled in sleek modernity. They exercised compassion on their captive peoples, allowing the Jews to return to Jerusalem under Ezra and Nehemiah, for instance. And they were ecumenical in their religious tolerance. Only in their hunger for military might and territorial conquest was their fierceness revealed.

At its zenith, their empire was the largest of the ancient world, covering almost double the territory of Assyria. Their wealth, too, outstripped anything else the world had ever seen. In addition, they were able to maintain control over their domain for nearly two millennia, save for the rude interruption of the Mongols during the thirteenth century.

Although technically part of the Middle East, the Persian kings distinguished themselves from their Arab brethren. They preserved their Farsi language rather than adopting the Arabic common to all of the other nations in the region. They emphasized their refined urban culture over and above the rough-and-tumble Bedouin mentality of their neighbors. And even after they were converted to Islam from Zoroastrianism during the seventh century, they maintained their dualistic mysticism and became the influential revolutionary center for both the Shi'ite and the Wahhabi sects of fundamental Islam. As the ruling Pahlevi shahs often asserted, the Persians were "a people apart."

Despite the constitutional establishment of modern Iran after World War I in place of the old Persia, the imperial ambitions of the people did not wane. They longed for the glory of the bygone era. They chafed against the yoke of Third World mediocrity. Then, providentially, the stream of wealth that came from Persian Gulf oil enabled them to stoke the fires of pride once again.

Thus, between 1967 and 1971, the shah staged a series of Persian celebrations, including a lavish imperial coronation for himself, during a five-year-long observance of the 2,500th anniversary of the reign of Cyrus from Persepolis. These affairs turned out to be the most extravagant the modern world had ever witnessed—certainly worthy of the heir of Cyrus, Xerxes, Darius, and Artaxerxes!

The mantle that the shah wore during the festivities was a gift from the people of Meshed and Khnassan. The long white cashmere garment was emblazoned with peacock feathers sewn with gold thread and pearls, and the edges, pockets, and sleeves were encrusted with gold and silver palettes. The pearls alone weighed almost five pounds. The closing at the neck was an aigrette of diamonds set around one large emerald and five smaller, pear-shaped rubies—the gems arranged to resemble flags, banners, and ancient armaments. This extraordinary confection weighed nearly eight hundred carats. Around his waist the monarch wore a belt of gold mail with a buckle set with a huge two-hundred-carat emerald surrounded by sixty brilliants and nearly one hundred fifty diamonds. His gold scepter, a gift from the people of Azerbaijan, was surmounted by a globe with three lions, three suns, and a crown of gold set with precious stones. His golden sword was slid into a sheath set with countless emeralds, rubies, sapphires, and more than twelve thousand diamonds. And his crown had more than three thousand diamonds, four hundred pearls, and a scattering of emeralds and sapphires.

Nearly two hundred acres of the ruins at Persepolis had been restored for the celebrations, great hangings of embossed purple velvet and gilt bronze friezes adorning every surface. The shah was transported around the grounds in an ebony carriage encrusted with mother-of-pearl and stamped with the royal Persian crest. The dais that he sat upon was a replica of the famed peacock throne of Xerxes, made of gold-plated acacia wood set with nearly thirty thousand precious gemstones.

On one occasion nine kings, five queens, thirteen princes, eight princesses, sixteen presidents, three prime ministers, two governors-general, nine sheiks, and two sultans—more accumulated royalty than at any other time in history except at the funeral of Edward VII in 1910—gathered together for a grand banquet. The shah served them a remarkable Persian feast of quail eggs stuffed with caviar, lobster mousse with Nantua sauce, flaming lambs with arrack, roast peacock stuffed with foie gras, platters of cheese, a salad of figs and raspberries, champagne sherbet, twenty-five thousand bottles of wine, and a single seventy-pound cake.

Like the festival of Saddam Hussein in Babylon and the fete of Hafez al Assad in Deir ez Zur, the shah's royal gala was designed to set the course for the future of the nation according to the compass of the past. According to the shah, "The glory of Persia is merely represented in the embellishments you see about you. In fact, the essence of that glory is yet to be fully realized as our nation only now begins to assume its proper place among the great nations of the earth. Persia shall arise."[5]

After the shah was deposed by the stern and ascetic Ayatollah Ruhollah Khomeini in 1979, it would have seemed logical that such imperial ambitions—and certainly such imperial opulence—would have been altogether shunned. But while the Ayatollah's revolution renounced the corruption of the shah, it actually embraced the ideal of Persian hegemony—or Islamic universalism. For instance, on his visit to the great reinforced vault in the basement of the Bank Melli, where the shah had kept the royal Persian treasury along with his own imperial baubles, the Ayatollah asserted,

Now in the hands of the Mullahs and Talabehs, these symbols of our great heritage shall give new impetus to the export of our revolution. Soon the spirit of Allah will sweep the faithful Umma of the Persian hoards across the earth: first, Jerusalem will be liberated for prayer; then, the Great Satan will be humiliated and crushed; and finally, our *Ji'had* will free the oppressed masses on every continent.[6]

On another occasion he said, "Our land has always been the seed-bed of true freedom—even before the Prophet came to correct the errors of time. Once again Persia shall lead the world as before. Conquest through *Ji'had* shall be our deliverance and our glory."[7]

Thus, archaeological exploration and restoration have continued unabated since the Ayatollah's revolution. If anything, the activity at various Persian ruins has increased. The Imams recognize only too well that an understanding of the past is the key to an understanding of the future.

Afghanistan

Afghanistan, 250,000 square miles of often forbidding terrain pinched between Iran and Pakistan, has been controlled by the radical Islamic Taliban movement since 1996. Negotiating—even communicating—with the Taliban has vexed governments and international organizations ever since the rag-tag cadre of former theology students brutally seized power after a long civil war. Only three countries—Pakistan, Saudi Arabia, and the United Arab Emirates—recognized the legitimacy of the Taliban.

The group, whose name means "seekers of spiritual knowledge," sprang up from ultraconservative Islamic schools in refugee camps in Pakistan. The camps were recruiting grounds for guerrilla groups during the Soviet Union's 1979–89 occupation of Afghanistan and during years of battle between rival ethnic warlords that followed the collapse of the Soviet-backed government in 1992.

Once in power, the Taliban ruthlessly suppressed all dissent, imposed a draconian standard of obedience to the dictates of the Koran, and systematically cut the nation off from the rest of the world. The nation became a pariah state with no legal economy—the only cash flow came from its booming poppy, opium, and heroin trade—no agricultural base, and no industrial infrastructure. More than one-third of all its citizens were able to survive only because they were fed daily by international aid workers.

It was hardly the first time the Afghan people had suffered at the hands of tyrants. The once rich and beautiful land had been the favored battleground for dozens of imperial conquerors, warlords, and viziers. Being a land bridge between the Asian subcontinent and the Russian steppes meant that it was a vital staging area for every ambitious general and every expanding empire.

By the middle of the sixth century B.C. the Persian Empire of the Achaemenid dynasty controlled most of what today is Afghanistan. But about 330 B.C., Alexander the Great defeated the last Achaemenid ruler and made his way to the eastern limits of Afghanistan and beyond. After his death in 323 B.C., several kingdoms fought for control of his Asian empire.

By about the first century A.D. the Kushans, a fierce Central Asian people, won control of the territory. Hinduism and Buddhism were the dominant religions for the next seven centuries, and a great pilgrimage road was cut through the land from India through Afghanistan and on into Central Asia.

Kushan power was destroyed first by Turkic White Huns or Ephthalites and then by the Arab armies of Muhammad's immediate successors. A series of Islamic regencies followed—first the Samanids, then the Ghaznavids, and finally the Ghurids. But in 1220 the Mongol conqueror Genghis Khan practically swallowed the realm whole. He in turn was followed a century later by the Asian warlord Tamerlane. Each conqueror left his mark on Afghanistan in devastation, destruction, and deprivation. Nevertheless, the rugged people remained proud, independent, and unbowed.

A descendant of Tamerlane on his father's side and Genghis Khan on his mother's side, Babur Zahiruddin Muhammad took Kabul in 1504 and established the foundations for the Afghan Mughal Empire. Only nominally Islamic, the empire lasted in one form or another until the nineteenth century when Afghanistan's strategic location became an irresistible linchpin to the imperial ambitions of European powers like Britain and Russia. It was only then that Islamic fundamentalism predominated among the Afghan people.

The Taliban's greatest inspiration for their repressive regime comes from the likes of Genghis Khan, Tamerlane, and Babur—only the last of whom was a Muslim. Muhammad Omar, the supreme leader of the Taliban, often invokes their example when stirring his fellow Mullahs to resist the *Kafir* Jews and their American sponsors:

> Praise be Allah, and prayers and peace upon Muhammad. We must rally ourselves in the strength and the name of Allah, the only wise, to resist the foes of Islam: the infidels, and the traitors. We must rise up, even as the great Khan, the mighty Tamerlane, and the honored Babur. We must imbibe their spirit of ferocity, and restore their reign of glory.[8]

For the strictly fundamentalist Afghanistan, as in the case of Iraq, Syria, and Iran, the lure of the past, even the infidel past of paganism, is alluringly invoked as part and parcel of its new Islamic vision.

Islamic Ambitions

In Islamic Iraq: a celebration of the spirit of pagan Babylon. In Islamic Syria: a celebration of the spirit of pagan Assyria. In Islamic Iran: a celebration of the spirit of pagan Persia. In Islamic Afghanistan: a celebration of the spirit of pagan Khans. And the pattern is repeated in other orthodox Islamic communities: Egypt, Libya, Sudan, Algiers, Pakistan, Indonesia, and Saudi Arabia.

At first glance, it would seem that the spirit of ancient paganism with its odd mixture of greed, tyranny, idolatry, and occultism would be roundly condemned by the clerical Imams, the Talabehs, the Mullahs, the Mu'adhdhun, or the Ayatollahs. But, in fact, two of the most passionate and fundamental ambitions of Islam enabled and even compelled them to embrace the primordial paganism of Babylon, Assyria, Persia, and Afghanistan.

The first ambition is Arab hegemony. Islamic tradition teaches that the faith revealed to Muhammad was not a new religion but was the oldest of all religions—an aboriginal and natural form of monotheism. According to the Koran, Islam is the original and unadulterated religion of the Middle East from which all other religions, including Judaism and Christianity, eventually developed. The ancient variants of this nascent Arabian mysticism in Babylon, Assyria, and Persia are thus popularly amalgamated into the universal heritage of Islam, despite distortions by virtue of the antiquity.

The symbolic polytheism of the Meccan region Hejaz, with the god Allah at the head of the pantheon, was absorbed by Muhammad into his Saracen system. Similarly the ancient and revered Ka'ba, the huge rectangular reliquary in the Meccan sanctuary, was transformed from a pagan temple into the focus of Muslim pilgrimage, the *Haj*. The stories of Abraham, Moses, and

Jesus were transferred from the Bible, with a number of strategic "corrections" and changes, directly into that Koran.

Through the years, such doctrinal borrowing has proliferated as pious Muslim scholars have attempted to discern the sundry palimpsests that led to the corruption of faith through the centuries—thus finding the essential core of Islamic truth in all religions.

There are many branches of Islam, some fundamentalist, some moderate, some liberal, and some conservative. But all of them share in this propensity to borrow from other faiths. For instance, the Sunnis—the largest branch of Islam and the one that Egyptian president Hosni Mubarak subscribes to—have adopted the pietism and oligarchism from the Greek Platonists. The Shi'ites— the branch of Islam that Muhammad Khatami of Iran subscribes to—have adopted occultation and channeling from the Jewish Kabbalists. The Sufis—the branch of Islam that Saddam Hussein subscribes to—have adopted antinomianism and mystical dualism from the Zoroastrians. The Alawites—the branch of Islam that Bashar al Assad of Syria subscribes to—have adopted reincarnation and thetanism from the Hindus. The Takfirs—the branch of Islam that Kuwait's Emir Jaber al Ahmed subscribes to—have adopted positivism and materialism from the Nestorians. And the Wahhabis—the branch of Islam that King Fahd of Saudi Arabia subscribes to—have adopted pragmatism and determinism from the Monophysites.

Despite this modicum of eclecticism, Islam has remained remarkably untainted by lax moral or doctrinal standards. By and large it is conservatively puritanical. Instead of being shaped by these outside influences, it has subsumed them into its universal hegemony and extended its legacy by baptizing them by proxy.

The second ambition of Islam that enables it to claim the legacy of ancient empires for itself is *Ji'had,* holy war, or *Dar al Harb.* According to Islamic tradition, the complete military subjugation of the earth is mandated by Allah. The conquests by the Muslims' Babylonian, Assyrian, Persian, and Khan forebears provide a living paradigm for their present task.

In the Hadith, Muhammad said, "Hear, O *Muslims,* the meaning of life. Shall I not tell you of the peak of the matter, its pillar, and its topmost part? The peak of the matter is Islam itself. The pillar is ritual *Rakatin* prayer. And the topmost part is *Ji'had*—holy war."[9]

The Medinese Suras likewise encouraged all the faithful to take up the sword or the martyr's robe with civil and social enforcement: "The *Umma* who stay at home—apart from those who suffer from a grave impediment—are not equal to those who fight for the cause of Allah with their goods and their persons. Allah has given to those who fight a higher rank. He has promised all a good reward; but far richer is the recompense of all who fight against the infidel for him."[10]

The Suras go on to assure the believers that Allah is with them and will honor their sacrifice: "Prophet, rouse the faithful to arms. If there are twenty steadfast men among you, they shall vanquish two hundred; and if there are a hundred, they shall rout a thousand of the infidels, for they are devoid of understanding."[11]

Jews and Christians are specifically singled out as the primary targets of this *Ji'had:* "Fight against such of those to whom the Scriptures were given as believe not in Allah. They must be utterly subdued for they worship their rabbis and their monks as gods."[12]

The remarkable success of the empires of the ancient Middle East provides encouragement and impetus for Muslims to faithfully carry out the command to wage holy war. The weight of glory is great. Islam thus needs the foundational support of the distant past. And so, the legacy of Babylon, Assyria, Persia, and the Khans, as incongruous as it may seem, is happily embraced in the name and the spirit of Allah.

Learning the Lessons of History

At the State Department in Washington, talk of strategic initiatives or troop movements or diplomatic maneuvers is likely to attract keen interest. On the other hand, talk of the spiritual and historical forces that invigorate those strategic initiatives or motivate those troop movements or dominate those diplomatic maneuvers is likely to cause all too many eyes to glaze over.

It is not only the militant affinity of modern Islam with the primordial spiritual ambition of Babylon, Assyria, Persia, and the Khans that underlies the current East-West crisis; it is also the inability, and perhaps even the refusal, of the West to *deal* with that militant affinity.

If we continue to ignore the spiritual dimensions of this conflict, we will be wrecked upon the shoals of history just as surely as Babylon, Assyria, Persia, and the Khans once were. It is an ancient script now unfolding in the Middle East: "Do you have eyes but fail to see, and ears but fail to hear? And don't you remember?" (Mark 8:18 NIV).

Chapter Five

The Doubt of Abraham

In one sense, Babylon is the acceptance of matter as the only meaning, the source of all mystery. That man could accept the shell for the total meaning, that his vanity could lead him to believe that he could control matter and hence life, is the ultimate folly. It is the perennial sickness of sin. It is the great conflict of Ishmael over and against Isaac.

—ANDREW NELSON LYTLE[1]

As the *muezzin* began the haunting call to prayer on the morning of October 8, 1990, some three thousand of the faithful gathered in front of the Al Aqsa mosque on *Haram es Sherif*, Jerusalem's famed Temple Mount. But instead of quietly making their way into the mosque, the *Umma*, the true believers of Islam, began to stockpile rocks, bricks, bottles, scraps of iron, and other makeshift weapons.

Forty feet below, nearly twenty thousand Jewish pilgrims and tourists, entirely oblivious to the disaster brewing up on the Mount, were celebrating Sukkoth at the Wailing Wall.

Suddenly cries of "Allah Akbar" (Allah is great), "Ji'had" (holy war), and "Itbakh al Yahud" (slaughter the Jews) erupted over the mosque's loudspeakers. A well-orchestrated assault then began.

The stockpiled weapons were hurled down upon the heads of the Jewish worshipers. A small police outpost on the Mount was burned to the ground. Huge boulders were rolled across nearby intersections to prevent police reinforcements from entering the area. And an unruly mob of teenagers ransacked the shops and stores in adjacent neighborhoods.

The melee lasted nearly an hour. About forty Israeli policemen tried to disperse the rioters with tear gas and rubber bullets, but to no avail. The enraged Muslims fought back with axes and chains. Rocks continued to rain down from the Mount. The streets of the Old City were rife with rioters.

Finally the police resorted to live ammunition. When the dust cleared, twenty-one Muslims lay dead, and the crisis in the Middle East had just escalated out of control. Another cheerless chapter was about to be written in the eternal blood feud between Ishmael and Isaac—one that would unleash a rash of suicide bombings and terror spilling out from Israel and Palestine onto the entire world stage.

Ishmael and Isaac

Abraham was known as a man of faith. But the fruit of his doubt has most shaped the spiritual and geopolitical crisis in the Middle East today.

God promised him an heir. When he came up out of Ur in the land of the Chaldees, God told him that through that heir, the nations would be blessed. Through that heir, mighty people would be raised up who would be the focal point of faith, hope, and love the world over. Abraham believed, and thus became the "friend of God."

But that promised heir was not forthcoming. Years passed, then decades. As the time slowly wore on, Abraham began to have subtle doubts. He began to fear that he had perhaps misunderstood God's promise. Sarah, his wife, was barren, and both were becoming quite elderly. The possibility of a natural heir seemed increasingly impossible. So he and Sarah decided to take matters into their own hands.

In some parts of the ancient Middle East, it was obligatory for a barren wife to provide her husband with an indentured concubine who would bear children for her by proxy. Legally the children were to be the issue of the wife, not the servant. In their doubt, Abraham and Sarah resorted to this surrogacy scheme, and a child was conceived. They named him Ishmael.

Fourteen years later, they saw how foolish they had been ever to doubt God's promise. A child was born to Sarah at the age of ninety. The natural heir they had yearned for was theirs. They named him Isaac.

Conflict between these two sons of Abraham began almost from the start. One was "born according to the flesh," and the other was "born according to the Spirit" (Gal. 4:29). The one, disinherited by the other, apparently became bitter, "mocking" and "persecuting" his half brother. Eventually the situation became so intolerable that Sarah demanded that Ishmael and his Egyptian concubine mother Hagar be expelled from the family to wander in the desert (Gen. 21:9–21).

That was not the end of the matter. It was only the beginning.

According to the Bible, Ishmael went to live in the wilderness of Paran, in the region of Hejaz (Gen. 25:18). There he had twelve patriarchal sons, as did both of his nephews, Jacob and Esau. Scripture associates the clans and tribes descended from him with the Midianites, the Edomites, the Egyptians, and the Assyrians (Gen. 37:36; 28:9; 25:18). This concurs with Islamic tradition, which asserts that Ishmael settled in the city of Mecca, which eventually became the capital of Hejaz and the holy city of Islam. There he became the unquestioned leader of all the diverse peoples throughout the Middle East.

Meanwhile, Isaac begat a long line of faithful men—Jacob, Joseph, Moses, Joshua, Gideon, and David—who were able to claim the full inheritance of Abraham: the land of Israel.

From Isaac came the Jews.

From Ishmael came the Arabs.

And the two have been at enmity with one another ever since.

The First Palestinian Conflict

Israel is the promised land of the Jews (Gen. 12:7). It is their Abrahamic inheritance (Gen. 15:18–21). But throughout history, they have inhabited it only rarely.

When Moses secured freedom from slavery in Egypt for his people, he led them back to that patriarchal homeland. They had been absent four hundred years. During that time, others had inhabited the region. The Canaanites, Ammonites, Edomites, Moabites, Midianites, and Philistines had made their homes in and around Palestine, and they were hardly inclined to recognize Israel's prior claim. In addition, the original settlers—the Kenites, Kenizzites, Kadmonites, Hittites, Perizzites, Rephaim, Girgashites, and Jebusites—were equally uncooperative. War between Ishmael and Isaac was inevitable.

According to the Bible, the conquest of the land under the leadership of heroes of faith and valor such as Joshua, Caleb,

Othniel, Ehud, Shamgar, Deborah, Gideon, Jephthah, Samson, Samuel, Saul, and David was a long, bloody, and torturous affair not to be forgotten by either side. Ever.

The *Sahih Muslim* annals written during the time of Muhammad's *Hijra* in Medina assert,

> The criminal Jews have brought destruction upon the *Umma* since the earliest times. Their leaders conspired to send the innocent of Canaan away from their homes. They repulsed the pleas of the Philistine widows and Moabite orphans and washed their fields in the blood of the Ammonite poor. Therefore, they shall not stand in the Day of Judgment, nor shall they prevail against the sure coming of *Ji'had*. Allah shall pronounce just retribution and the *Umma* shall observe with joy and gladness.[2]

Several years before he signed the extraordinary Camp David Accord with Israel, Egyptian President Anwar Sadat said, "The assassination of Arab brethren, like Goliath, by Jewish sheepherders like David, is the sort of shameful ignominy that we must yet set aright in the domain of the occupied Palestinian homeland."[3]

About the same time, Palestinian leader Yasser Arafat declared:

> Be assured that the many indignities heaped upon the Palestinian people since ancient times must and shall be avenged. Israel's policy in the occupied territories is little more than an extension of the imperialist tactics of the conqueror Joshua. Surely the judgment of Allah is reserved for them until Palestine is transferred from *Dar al Harb* to *Dar al Islam*. Ishmael shall have his revenge.[4]

Following the demise of the kingdoms of Israel and Judah at the hands of the Assyrians and Babylonians, it seemed that Ishmael had his revenge. But then the Persians restored Isaac to Palestine, and the ancient rivalry was resumed, beginning with Tobiah and Sanballat's challenge of Ezra and Nehemiah.

The advent of Greek and Roman imperial rule quelled the fires of hatred for a time. Stability was forcibly imposed on the Middle East by the legions of the West until the Roman armies laid waste to Palestine, crushing the aspirations of both Ishmael and Isaac.

Suddenly they were back to square one.

The Second Palestinian Conflict

Most of the Jews who survived the destruction of Jerusalem and the devastation of the land at the hands of the Romans in A.D. 70 joined the already large Diaspora in exile. But a few continued to try to scratch out a living in the blighted environs of Palestine.

During the period of Roman—and later Byzantine—rule, Palestine was utterly neglected. Its poverty became abject. The once lush gardens and fertile fields were left to the scourge of the harsh elements. Trees and vegetation were cut away with profligate indulgence. What little remained of the once beautiful architecture deteriorated badly due to neglect. Even so, the Jews were legally protected, and they could work and worship in relative peace and security. And because the entire Arab population had converted to Christianity, Palestine became a tiny Jewish island in the vast sea of the Christian Middle East.

But then came Islam.

During the time that he was exiled from Mecca, Muhammad launched a fierce *Ji'had* against the significant Jewish communities of Hejaz. In Medina, the interim headquarters of his nascent movement, he had the Jewish men scourged and decapitated in the public square. He then divided their women, children, animals, and property among his followers.

During this time he recorded in his Koranic revelations the immutability of the eternal conflict between Muslims and Jews:

You shall surely find the most violent of all men in enmity against the *Umma* to be the Jews. (5:82)

O, true believers, take not the Jews and Christians for your friends. They cannot be trusted. They are defiled—filth. (5:51)

The Jews are smitten with vileness and misery and drew on themselves indignation from Allah. (2:61)

Wherever they are found, the Jews reek of destruction—which is their just reward. (3:112)

According to the Meccan chronicles of that early period, recorded in the *Sahih Muslim* annals, all Jews were anathema and were to be annihilated: "Allah's messenger—may peace be upon him—has commanded: Fight against the Jews and kill them. Pursue them until even a stone would say: Come here, Muslim, there is a Jew hiding himself behind me. Kill him. Kill him quickly."

For the first time in centuries, the old feud between Ishmael and Isaac had been revived.

As he gained more and more control over the Arabian Peninsula and then over the entire Mediterranean world, Muhammad tempered his policy of wholesale slaughter. Expediency dictated that much. Many of the hated Jews proved to be valuable assets to his administration. Some had professional skills and resources. Others had economic skills and resources. Thus, he began to find it politic to invent a kind of treaty, or *Dhimma*, merely to subjugate his beaten foes, sparing their lives in exchange for a tithe of half their property, to be levied in perpetuity. Christians and even Jews were spared as long as they continued to contribute to the ongoing support of *Ji'had* with the substance of their wealth.

Eventually *Dhimma* became more sophisticated. The subject peoples were given the right to live and to practice their religion on a limited basis. They even received protection in return for payment of special taxes: the *Kharaj*, or land tax; the *Ji'zya*, or poll tax; the *Fad'lak*, or travel tax; and the *Sult'ah*, or special taxes levied at the ruler's pleasure. The problem was that the status of the captive people was always at risk, since the *Dhimma* merely suspended the conqueror's Koranic right to kill them and confiscate their property. It could be revoked at the slightest whim.

Muhammad died in A.D. 632. But the scourge of *Ji'had* and *Dhimma* had only begun. Over the next decade, Muhammad's successors, Caliph Abu Bakr and Caliph Umar, were able to consolidate their military control over all of Arabia, from the Hejaz to Najd and from Asir to al Hasa. They conquered most of Sassanid Iraq and Byzantine Egypt. They made serious advances against Syria that permanently destabilized that important Christian province. And by 638, they had conquered Palestine as well.

Thousands of Jews were slaughtered along with the Byzantine Christians. A few of the most technically proficient Jews continued to live under the Muslim domination of *Dhimma*—Baghdad, Kairouan, and Umayyad Spain boasted strong Jewish professional communities—but most of the rest fled into uneasy exile in Christian Europe. In any case, Palestine was emptied of its indigenous population once again, and the conflict between Ishmael and Isaac was made moot. Again. But only for a little while.

The Third Palestinian Conflict

Zionism was born in Europe among well-educated Jewish professionals who had finally come to realize that absorption into Western culture was utterly impossible. It seemed to them that the path to acceptance was hopelessly blocked by prejudice or avarice or perhaps worldview incompatibility.

After centuries of persecution, hardship, humiliation, pogroms, ghettoes, and purges, the nineteenth century had brought them to the place of almost universal emancipation. But even with official legal restrictions removed, the unofficial cultural animus of anti-Semitism in Europe continued to wield overwhelming force.

The Jews began to dream once again about the possibility of returning home from their long-imposed Diaspora. They began to dream once again of Zion.

The Zionist ideal was not entirely new, of course. For nearly two millennia, wherever there was a community of Jews, some yearned for a return to Erez Israel. And ambitious European politicians and monarchs often proposed a resettled Jewish state in Palestine as a possible solution to various difficulties both at home and in the decrepit Middle East. But with the writings of Moses Hess, Emanuel Deutsch, Benjamin Disraeli, Emma Lazarus, and George Eliot a whole new notion was conceived: a secular Jewish state.

And then came Theodor Herzl.

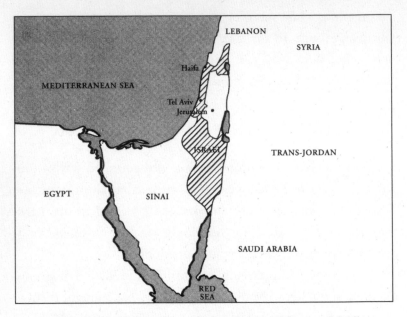

The United Nation Partition Plan, 1947

Herzl was a journalist for the liberal Vienna daily *Neue Freie Presse*. While covering the shameful trial of Alfred Dreyfus, a French army officer wrongly accused of treason and mercilessly vilified on racial grounds, Herzl experienced a dramatic conversion of the soul. He became an ardent Zionist. Zionism became his driving passion. He lived it and breathed it. Within months he transformed what had been little more than wishful thinking for centuries into a political movement. His book, *Der Judenstaat*, became the lightning rod for two generations of Jews who had struggled, fought, bled, and died to realize their ambition.

Inspired by Herzl's vision and supported by a worldwide network of Zionist organizations, Jewish families began to return to Palestine, buying up small tracts of barren deserts and abandoned ruins from the doddering Ottoman overseers. After World War I,

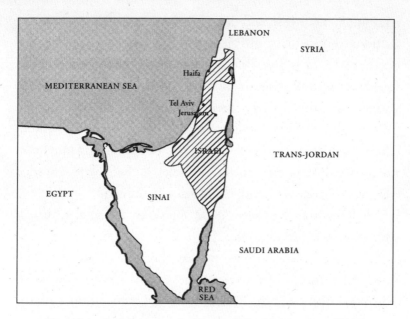

Furthest Lines of Israeli Advance, 1948

when the British assumed responsibility for the administration of the region, first a small trickle and then a steady stream of Jewish settlers made their way out of the lands of persecution back to Zion. After World War II, when the horrors of the Holocaust were revealed to the world, a literal flood of exiles returned from the Diaspora.

For the first time in centuries, Ishmael and Isaac lived in proximity to one another. And not surprisingly tensions flared almost immediately.

The British tried desperately to appease both sides. The Balfour Declaration in 1917 committed the government to supporting the Zionist cause, but concerns for the indigenous Arab population caused them to recalcitrantly waffle. A bitter cycle of demonstrations, strikes, riots, terrorism, and reprisals followed— on both sides of the conflict—for more than three decades. In frustration, the British and the newly constituted United Nations partitioned the district of Palestine. They designated the western one-fourth as a Jewish Palestinian state and the eastern three-fourths as an Arab Palestinian state and then gave the two new nations autonomy. Their intention was to settle the question once and for all. Their intention was to bring peace to the region. Their intention was to give the people of both Trans-Jordan, as the new Arab state was called, and Israel, as the new Jewish state was called, freedom, security, and self-determination.

All those intentions were good. But even the road to hell is paved with good intentions.

The day after Israel officially became a nation, May 14, 1948, three Palestinian Arab armies—the Najada Forces, the Arab Liberation Army, and the Futuwa Defense League, along with the national military forces of Lebanon, Syria, Egypt, Jordan, Iraq, and several contingents from the Saudi Arabian Army—launched a bitter war for control of the entire Palestinian region.

According to the Arab leaders, there was absolutely no possibility for any sort of compromise or negotiated peace.

Haj Amin el Husseinin, the *Mufti* of Jerusalem who had served the Nazis during World War II and who now led the Palestinian Arab resistance, declared, "The entire Jewish population in Palestine must be destroyed or be driven into the sea. Allah has bestowed upon us the rare privilege of finishing what Hitler only began. Let the *Ji'had* begin. Murder the Jews. Murder them all."[5]

King Abdul Aziz Ibn Saud, the founding monarch of the Saudi sultanate, said, "The Arab nations should sacrifice up to ten million of their fifty million people, if necessary, to wipe out Israel. Israel to the Arab world is like a cancer to the human body. And the only way of remedy is to uproot it."[6] Likewise, Al Riyadh Saud said, "The power struggle between Israel and the Arabs is a long-term historical trial. Victory or defeat are for us questions of existence or annihilation, the outcome of an irreconcilable hatred."[7]

Azzam Pasha, secretary general of the Arab League, asserted that "this will be a war of extermination and a momentous massacre which will be spoken of like the Mongolian massacres and the Crusades. No Jew will be left alive."[8] King Farouk of Egypt concurred: "The Jews in Palestine must be exterminated. There can be no other option for those of us who revere the name of Allah. There will be no *Dhimma*. There will only be *Ji'had*."[9]

From King Abdullah of Trans-Jordan to Zahir Shah of Afghanistan, from Imam Yahya of Yemen to King Hassan of Morocco, from Reza Shah of Iran to Regent Abd al Ilah of Iraq, every Muslim leader in the Middle East called for the destruction of Israel and the execution of the Jews. Even the moderate King Idris of Libya sounded the call for genocide: "The Zionist conquest of Palestine is an affront to all Muslims. This colonialist barbarism cannot and will not be tolerated. There can be no compromise until every Jew is dead and gone."[10]

Israeli leaders responded tenaciously that they would fight to the death to keep and defend their new landholdings, and they swore that one day they would occupy Jerusalem as well. Terror spawned terror.

Although the war ended in a stalemate—with Israel keeping most of the territory it was allotted in the partition plus some—the animosity between Ishmael and Isaac intensified. Successive wars in 1956, 1967, and 1973 made their conflict a global concern. In addition, the terrorist strikes of the Palestine Liberation Organization (PLO) and the portrayed involvement of Israel in the Lebanese civil war only aggravated the open wounds of dis-

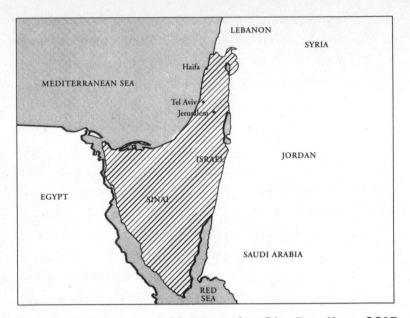

Israeli territory following the Six Day War, 1967

possession, anarchy, and geopolitical strife. Violence and strife have become a regular part of the Palestinian landscape—as familiar as the Judean hills.

And still, the hatred is unabated.

Sheikh Tamimi, the last *Mufti* of Jerusalem, who was responsible for organizing the ill-fated Temple Mount uprising, issued a call for all Muslims to join arms against Israel at a time when it seemed that the Gulf War and its international coalition arrayed against Iraq might permanently disrupt Islamic unity: "The Jews are destined to be persecuted, humiliated, and tortured forever, and it is a Muslim duty to see to it that they reap their due. No petty arguments must be allowed to divide us. Where Hitler failed we must succeed."[11]

Yasser Arafat, the longtime chairman of the PLO and the mastermind behind the *Intifada* uprising in the West Bank and Gaza Strip, has said again and again: "Our objective is simply the liberation of the Palestinian soil and the establishment of a Palestinian state over every part of it. Thus, the Jews must be removed and Israel must be annihilated. We can accept nothing less."[12]

Hafez al Assad, the dictator of Syria for the better part of two decades, agreed: "We shall never call for nor accept peace. We shall only accept war. We have resolved to drench this land with Israel's blood, to oust the Jews as aggressors, and to throw them all into the sea."[13]

In the face of this animosity, a number of Israeli leaders have responded in kind by authorizing new settlements to the occupied territories won from Jordan, Syria, and Egypt in the 1967 Six Day War, limiting the movement and civil liberties of Palestinian Arabs, and inhibiting economic opportunities for minority populations.

As a result of this intractable conflict, every problem in the Middle East is now somehow connected to the Palestinian question. For instance, when Saddam Hussein overran Kuwait in 1990, he blamed the conflict on Israel. When Hafez al Assad completed his conquest of Lebanon that same year, he blamed the crisis on Israel. When Muammar Qaddafi of Libya sparked a coup in Chad, also in 1990, he blamed the situation on Israel. When Khalid al Alhamzi of Sudan launched a systematic program of genocide against the country's own Christian population in the south, he blamed it all on Israel. When Osama bin Laden unleashed his reign of terror on the innocent civilians of the United States, he justified his actions by laying the blame squarely at the door of Israel. This seemingly absurd linkage has become inescapable.

Hashemi Rafsanjani of Iran explained:

Every problem in our region can be traced to this single dilemma:

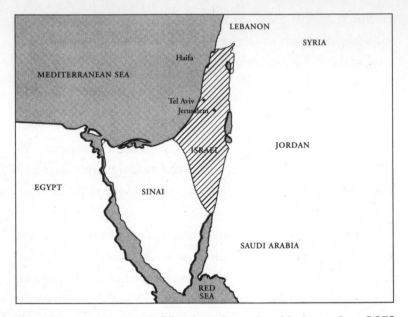

Israeli territory following Camp David Accords, 1978

the occupation of *Dar al Islam* by Jewish infidels or Western imperialists. Every political controversy, every boundary dispute, and every internal conflict is spawned by the inability of the *Umma* to faithfully and successfully wage *Ji'had.* The everlasting struggle between Ishmael and Isaac cannot cease until one or the other is utterly vanished.[14]

And so the conflict continues. The blood of Abraham continues to be spilled with prodigal abandon.

Doubt's Legacy

Clearly the conflict between the Jews and the Muslims is not a question of borders or settlements or political self-determination. Thus, it cannot be solved by manipulating the political apparatus. It is an intractable spiritual problem. And it must be dealt with in spiritual terms:

> Though we walk in the flesh, we do not war according to the flesh. For the weapons of our warfare are not carnal but mighty in God for pulling down strongholds, casting down arguments and every high thing that exalts itself against the knowledge of God, bringing every thought into captivity to the obedience of Christ. (2 Cor. 10:3–5 NKJV)

To approach the current East-West crisis in any other fashion is to invite disaster. That, of course, is not to say that we are to become so heavenly minded that we are of no earthly good. It is to say, however, that we cannot deal with a problem effectively if we treat only the symptoms and ignore the root causes.

And the root causes in the Middle East are first and foremost spiritual, not military, strategic, or diplomatic.

Chapter Six

Unholy *Ji'had*

Though we tend to admire courage, we often have to admit
that there is an unexplainable admixture of boldness and madness in it.

—TRISTAN GYLBERD[1]

On the morning of November 4, 1979, in the holy city of Qom,
the patriarch of the Shi'ite faith—the man many Muslims believed
to be either the long-awaited caliph of all Islam or perhaps the
prophesied incarnation of the occulted *Mahdi*—was seething with
righteous indignation. Allah's revolution of righteousness was in
danger, he told his small audience of Mullahs, Imams, and students. The enemies of Islam were attempting to undermine the liberation of the *Umma.* The Great Satan was at large right in their
midst. Something must be done, he said as he dismissed them. The
"nest of spies and infidels" must be eliminated.

Word spread quickly. Ayatollah Ruhollah Khomeini had
spoken.

Within a few hours, the small demonstration of young people
that regularly gathered outside the American Embassy on
Taleghani Street in Tehran, some eighty miles north of the
Ayatollah's humble residence, had grown into a swarming mob.

105

Before noon, they had burst into the compound, chanting, "Death to America!" "Death to the infidels!" "Death to the Great Satan!" "Ji'had! Ji'had! Ji'had!"

The embassy personnel and their marine guards secured themselves in the chancellery building to wait for the Iranian police or the army to restore order. But they never came. By early afternoon the mob had taken the frightened Americans hostage.

But the full dimensions of the drama had yet to be revealed.

Early the next morning Seyyed Khomeini, the Ayatollah's son, visited the embassy and conferred with the militant captors. In a hastily called press conference at the gate of the compound he told the milling masses that he, like his father, supported the takeover.

Meanwhile, America looked on in horror and disbelief. Disturbing television footage of the hostages, bound and gagged and paraded about like game after a hunt, was beamed into millions of living rooms. Images of madcap street demonstrations of flailing, shouting, and cursing Muslim fanatics were etched on the nation's conscience. It was a nightmare come to life. Madness seemed to have overtaken the world.

The *Ji'had* had begun. Again.

The Infidels

During the formative years of his faith, Muhammad had very little contact with orthodox Christianity. He might have heard the stories from a few Christian merchants and caravanners who passed through the Hejaz on their way across the Arabian Peninsula from time to time. But those occasions were few and far between. Most of his understanding of the gospel was filtered through the twisted heresies of Arianism, Nestorianism, and Monophysitism.

That limited and skewed exposure contrasted sharply with his contact with Judaism. During his *Hijra*, or exile to Medina, he apparently had a series of acrimonious experiences with the Jewish community there. As a result, while the Koran hurls bitter invectives at the Jews, its condemnation of Christianity is rather mild.

Muhammad revered Jesus as "one of the prophets" (2:135). It was only a misunderstanding on the part of Christ's disciples, he contended, that led them to worship Him as the Son of God. They were, therefore, to receive special consideration as "people of the book" (29:46).

Nevertheless, they were infidels (2:140) and had to be dealt with as such. That meant that they were, unwittingly or not, guilty of shameful idolatry (6:20–23). They were thus subject to the judgment of God (22:17). And they were subject to the wrath of the *Umma*—the true community of Islam (9:4).

In other words, Christians were legitimate targets for the *Ji'had*, the holy war. Like the Jews, they were to be subjugated and brought under *Dhimma*, or they were to be killed. No other option was tolerable to the faithful Muslim:

Who will protect them, by night or by day, from the Lord of Justice? Yet they are unmindful of their Lord's remembrance. Have they any other means to protect them? Their idolatry will be powerless for their salvation. Nor shall they be protected from our scourge. Good things have been bestowed upon these men and upon their fathers. They have lived long and prospered. But now, we shall invade their lands and curtail their borders. Can they then triumph? They have been warned by inspiration, but the deaf can hear nothing. (21:41–46)

The *Ji'had* was to be pursued at all costs. Death was of no concern to the Muslim because, according to the Koran, those who died at the hands of the infidels during the *Ji'had* were actually martyrs, earning a certain and immediate entrance into paradise (3:156–59). In fact, martyrdom was considered to be the devotional pinnacle of *al Salaam*, or Islamic submission (3:167–75).

During the first four decades of the seventh century, Muslim armies began to engage the defenses of the Christian Middle East. With the divine assurance of ultimate victory and the comfort of devotional martyrdom inspiring them, Muslim troops threw themselves into battle with passion, vision, and potency. And more often than not, they won.

Byzantium

At that time, the far-flung Byzantine Empire had become a manifest monument to the beneficence of Christian culture. Throughout the Middle East, across North Africa, and deep into the heart of Europe, imperial stability and steadfastness had spawned a remarkable flowering of culture.

The legal system was just and efficient. Government was limited and decentralized. Trade was free and prosperous. Families were stable and secure. Perversity and corruption were suppressed while personal liberty and civil rights were enhanced. Advancement in the sciences was unprecedented. Art, music, and ideas flourished as in no other time in human history. And the literary output was bedazzling.

One visitor to the capital, Fulcher of Chartres, expressed complete awe at its vast achievements:

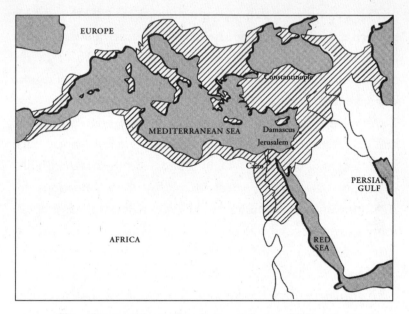

The Byzantine Empire, circa 560 A.D.

How splendid a civilization, how stately, how fair, how spiritually inclined, how many palaces raised by sheer labor in its highways and streets, how many works of art, marvelous to behold. It would be wearisome to tell of the abundance of all good things; of gold and silver, of charity and grace, of garments of varied appearance, and of sacredness unimaginable.[2]

Another visitor at the time, Maedock of Alliers, marveled at the general happiness of the Byzantine culture: "The evident misery in so many other domains is seemingly altogether absent here in the East. The prosperity and liberty enjoyed by all has had a melodious effect upon them. Industry and labor is undertaken with gladness of heart. Benediction is upon every tongue. Surely God's grace has rested upon them."[3]

The Byzantine church was quite robust as well. Evangelistic missionary endeavors had spread the gospel message from Scandinavia to China and from the depths of Africa to the steppes of Russia. Theological orthodoxy was ensured by regular creedal councils, canonical synods, and conciliar presbyteries that decentralized authority and power among several episcopacies and patriarchates. And local congregational vitality was catalyzed by an emphasis on strong preaching and a sacramental parish life.

Despite all these apparent strengths, the foundations for Byzantine unity had a number of hidden weaknesses. Most significantly the long-lived stability of the imperial order had encouraged a lax estimation of the importance of military preparedness.

When the Islamic armies first began to venture out of the Arabian desert, they quickly saw and exploited that weakness. Though often greatly outnumbered by Byzantine forces, the fearless, tenacious Muslims prevailed time after time. They swarmed almost suicidally onto the battlefield in vast human waves. Their valor was unreserved, their fervor untempered. Their malevolence was unrelenting, their passion unbridled. They fought not for themselves or their homelands or their ideology or their race. They fought for Allah. And they died for paradise. The Byzantine armies were entirely unprepared for such fervor, ardor, and zeal.

One imperial observer, Lameh Chrysostine, stated at the time: "It is almost as if they are driven by the very demons of Hell itself. They are in no wise tempted by comfort or safety. Instead, I dare say, they relish the ardor of battle and welcome the horrors of death."[4]

The caliph Umar—who led those early stinging campaigns along the southern frontier of Syria, into the fertile Mesopotamian valley of Iraq, along the Nile in Egypt, and ultimately into Palestine itself—was a stern giant of a man with a long dark beard and a full, brooding countenance. He wore coarse, frayed garments and always carried a whip in his right fist in order to enforce righteous humility among his men. He had little appreciation for the accomplishments of Byzantium and was single-minded in his desire to bring the empire to its knees.

According to the *Shah Nemeh,* a contemporary chronicle of caliphs and kings, Umar despised the Christian infidels for their "half-faith" and yearned to force their confessions, creeds, and liturgies into extinction:

> Umar—may he ever have peace—coveted nothing in the flesh save the undoing of Christian arrogance; for Jews are impotent and pagans are powerless; but in Christians he saw challenge. Therefore, his meat was their humiliation; his drink was their shame; his humor was their downfall; his very breathing was their destruction. To see the whole earth bow in submission to Allah was his sure desire; but to see Christendom fall was his great delight.[5]

Umar pursued that delight with vigor and proficiency. By A.D. 634, his armies had completed their conquest of Syria. By 635, he controlled much of Egypt. And by 636, he had defeated the Byzantines decisively in the great Battle of Yarmuk, thus attaining unchallenged authority throughout the Fertile Crescent.

But Umar was not content.

In February 638, he entered Jerusalem riding on a white camel. As always, he was dressed in his worn, filthy robes, and the army that followed him was rough and unkempt. Yet its discipline was

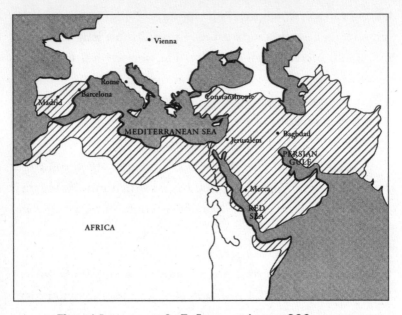

The Advance of Islam, circa 900 A.D.

perfect and its victory complete. The cardinal city of Christendom with all its shrines, relics, monasteries, and holy places was in the hands of Islam.

And still Umar was not content.

Before his death in 644, he had spread the dominion of Islam from the Euphrates across the North African Littoral. He had conquered all of Iraq, brought the Persians to the brink of collapse, controlled the southern Mediterranean coastline, and put Christendom on the defensive at every turn. In addition, he left his successors a tumultuous momentum that gave them expansive new conquests in Spain, Sicily, Crete, and Italy.

It was not until 733, when Charles Martel stopped the Muslim advance north of the Pyrenees, that this first great period of Islamic expansion came to an end. In just one hundred years, the map of the venerable old Mediterranean world had practically been transformed from one vast Christian empire into a vast Islamic one.

Though the *Ji'had* had not yet conquered the entire world, it was coming torturously and confidently close. The very existence of Byzantium seemed to hang by a mere thread.

The Crusades

The idea of some kind of a holy war to avenge the subjugation of Christian lands first occurred to Pope Gregory VII, and then to his successor Victor III, but affairs closer to home kept both more than a little preoccupied. Soon, though, stories of gross atrocities against captive churches reached the West. The brutal conquest of Egypt, Syria, and Iraq sent shudders of fear throughout the kingdoms of the West. The penetration of Muslim armies into Spain, France, and Italy and the slaughter of whole communities of believers shook their confidence even more. The vulnerability of the once invulnerable Byzantine Empire was utterly terrifying to them. And horrific stories of the occupation of the Holy Land—Jerusalem and Palestine—and the desecration of the sacred sites of the Christian faith there distressed them no end. They could no longer ignore such abscesses of despotism.

At the Council of Clermont in 1095, Pope Urban II issued a call for concerted and forthright action that was heard throughout Europe: "From the confines of Jerusalem and from the city of Constantinople a horrible tale has gone forth. An accursed race, a race utterly alienated from God, has invaded the lands of those Christians and depopulated them by the sword, plundering, and fire."[6] He went on to list in detail the outrages of the *Ji'had*: the plunder of churches, the rape of Christian women, the torture of

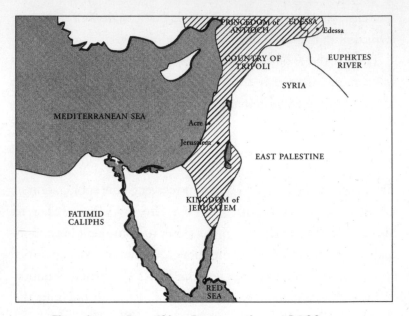

The Crusader Kingdoms, circa 1200 A.D.

priests and monks, the pilfering of villages and towns, and the occupation of the territories.

He appealed to their sense of Christian mercy and their sense of European honor:

Recall the greatness of Charlemagne. O most valiant soldiers, descendants of invincible ancestors, be not degenerate. Let all hatred between you depart, all quarrels end, all wars cease. Start upon the road to the Holy Sepulcher, to tear that land from a wicked race and subject it to yourselves thereby restoring it to Christ. I call you to take the cross and redeem defiled Jerusalem.[7]

Immediately a stirring chant arose from the crowd there at Clermont: "Deus Vult"—God wills it. It was a chant that would quickly spread throughout Europe. The following year, the Crusades began in earnest.

Few events in history have been more colored by romantic imagination than the Crusades. The very name conjures up a vision of gallant knights inspired by pure religious zeal, leaving home and country to embark on a just and holy war against crass infidel oppressors. In reality, the lure of booty, the mystery of the Orient, the promise of indulgences, the remission of penance, the aspiration to gain a feudal benefice, and a chaste sense of justice and chivalry all played their part among the intoxicating mixture of spiritual and fleshly motives that drew the nobles of Christian Europe into battle with the Imams of Muslim Asia.

But whatever their reasons, the knights and nobles who would eventually hear and heed that initial call to "take the cross" as a holy vow to redeem the East were the best that Christendom had to offer. They included Robert of Normandy, Raymond of Toulouse, Bohemond of Taranto, Robert of Flanders, Godfrey of Bouillon, Baldwin of Boulogne, and Stephen of Blois.

An army of about 50,000 Europeans, outfitted and supported by the Byzantines, relentlessly drove south through Syria and Palestine, finally retaking Jerusalem in 1099. For the first time in their short history, the Muslim horde fled in retreat. The bludgeon of the *Ji'had* and the *Dhimma* seemed to have been broken— at least for a time.

Outremer

During the next few years, the Crusaders carved up their conquests into several kingdoms and duchys—realms that they dubbed as Outremer. They built castles, churches, and markets. They constructed fortified walls, dug fresh wells, and cultivated the fields. They restored the holy places. They opened the trade routes. And they rebuilt the roadways.

Many of the men committed the rest of their lives to making the region a flourishing Christian culture once again. The feudal order that they instituted there brought dramatic changes to the lives and the fortunes of the citizenry. Under their ambitious building program, cities such as Acre, Edessa, and even Jerusalem itself blossomed into architectural marvels. Their obvious prosperity loomed large. Out of the rubble of war they wrought the fruits of peace.

But restoring the lands to their former glory was no easy task. Provisions had to be shipped across long distances. Communications with the West were difficult at best. Petty jealousies between competing clans, commanders, chiefs, and would-be czars weakened their solidarity, stalled their progress, and diverted their attentions. In the end there were not enough of them to hold their tiny strip of territory against the persistent onslaught of Muslim assassins, warlords, and potentates.

In 1144, the Saracens reorganized their armies and swept through Syria. Edessa fell. A renewed Crusade led by the kings of France and Germany failed to recover it. All of Europe was stunned. And the worst was yet to come.

In 1170, Saladin united the Islamic world under his leadership and began to chip away at the remaining Christian holdings. In 1187, he defeated the Crusaders at the decisive Battle of Hattin. He then captured Jerusalem and overran virtually all the Latin territories except Acre.

Such notables as King Richard I of England, Emperor Frederick

II of Germany, and King Louis IX of France launched another series of Crusades. Under their leadership the Western armies valiantly won back a few swatches of the lost lands between Joppa and Acre. But the flagging campaigns were generally ineffectual. Jerusalem was lost again in 1244, and Acre fell in 1291.

After that, the energies of pious Western princes unexpectedly and inexplicably turned to other concerns. Crusading remained a part of their feudal worldview, but instead of focusing on Outremer, they launched a whole host of Crusades against sundry European infidels:

- During the thirteenth century, the royal houses of France, Aragon, and Navarre led a Crusade in Toulouse against the Albigensians and Cathars.

- At about the same time the northern Italian republics led a Crusade against the Saracens in Naples and Sicily.

- During the thirteenth and fourteenth centuries the royal houses of Castile, Portugal, and Aragon led Crusades against the Moors in southern Iberia and along the northern coast of Africa.

- And during the fifteenth century the Teutonic knights led Crusades in Prussia and Lithuania against the Baltic Celts.

Each of these expeditions to consolidate the realms of Christendom was accompanied by papal indulgences and carried the full weight of holy war. The specter of the *Ji'had* and the *Dhimma* was all but forgotten as men "took the cross" for the sake of orthodoxy. But it would not be long before the slumbering giant of Islam would awaken to refresh their memories.

The Turkish Renewal

Christendom and Islam lived in unhappy but fairly stable coexistence for some time. But the separate peace was suddenly sundered with the advent of Turkish dominion throughout the East. The last remnants of Outremer colonial pride and Byzantine imperial glory were snuffed out of existence when this new and vital force swept through the Saracen realms from the north.

The Turks were the descendants of savage Saljuk tribesmen from the Mongol steppes. Their dramatic conversion to Islam in the eleventh century was followed by an unrivaled zeal to tangibly and aggressively realize Muhammad's original world and life view. As a result, their power and influence grew by leaps and bounds. By the beginning of the twelfth century, they had conquered the bulk of the Anatolian Plateau. In the thirteenth century they gained control of the caliphate and assumed authority over the military. And by the fourteenth century, they were ready to challenge the very existence of Christendom.

The Turks expanded their conquests at every turn. Like the armies of Umar before them, their hunger seemed utterly insatiable. The sultans called for a complete renewal of *Ji'had.* Western powers could no longer afford to trifle with petty Crusades along their borderlands. The Turks threatened their very existence. With the fall of Constantinople, that sober realization gripped them with vivid terror.

The Crusading Spirit

When the reality of the Turkish conquests was fully comprehended throughout Christendom, there was panic in the streets.

Economic fortunes were lost overnight. Political careers were destroyed. And whole theologies were suddenly cast into bankruptcy. The heathen had overrun the greatest symbol of Christian culture—and Europe's link to the mysteries of the East.

Doomsayers had a heyday. They predicted catastrophe and destruction. Experts on Bible prophecy began to expound new theories about a coming Great Tribulation and a terrible Apocalypse. Talk of the last days and the end times occupied the attention of Christians everywhere. Complex formulas were contrived to prove that the Antichrist and False Prophet had come and that the Great Whore of Babylon had been revealed. Charts were drawn up to show the increasing frequency and intensity of earthquakes, famines, and plagues. The "signs of the times" seemed to indicate that the countdown to Armageddon had actually begun.

But in other quarters, voices calling for the renewal of the Crusades made themselves heard above the din and clamor of eschatological confusion. The passion to "take the cross" was once again stirred in the souls of brave and pious men. Clerics preached the benefits of just and holy wars. Ambitious nobles cast their gaze across the eastern horizon with longing and wonder. Chivalric literature rose dramatically in popularity. The vows of old crusading orders and brotherhoods were renewed. And each pope during the last half of the fifteenth century made crusading a central tenet in his ecclesiastical and temporal policies:

- An early champion of Renaissance art, music, and ideas, Nicholas V also tried to rally Western princes to a military Crusade, issuing a papal bull on September 30, 1453—just four months after the fall of Byzantium—but a breakdown in the ongoing peace talks between Venice and Milan stymied any hope of concerted cooperation.

- Callistus III—the first of the controversial Borgias to rule in Rome—vowed to expend all his efforts and, if need be, his own life on the holy war. He dispatched legates armed with indulgences throughout Europe in 1456 and set about building a fleet to challenge Muslim superiority in the eastern Mediterranean. But aside from a few inconsequential skirmishes—near Belgrade on land and off Lesbos by sea—his efforts amounted to little.

- Pius II issued a Crusade bull shortly after ascending to the papal throne in 1458. He called for a congress of Christian rulers to meet at Mantua the next summer. Again, though, internecine conflicts prevented him from marching on Jerusalem.

- Paul II issued a general summons to a Crusade in 1470. But when he convened the Italian powers to a congress at Rome, all he could obtain was a defensive alliance against the Turks.

- Sixtus IV was enthusiastic for a Crusade against the Turks after the fall of Otranto in 1481. He spent lavishly equipping a fleet, but in spite of his appeals the European princes held back and the navy achieved only modest successes in the Aegean.

- The Genoese-born Innocent VIII focused most of his crusading attentions on the efforts of Ferdinand and Isabella to drive the Moors from the Iberian Peninsula. But he was also influential in securing funding for a number of other efforts aimed at retrieving territories lost to the Saracens, including the expedition of Columbus.

- Alexander VI—the flamboyant and controversial Borgia from Valencia—promised a reform of the curia and a united effort against the Turkish menace when he ascended the papal throne in 1492, but like those who had ruled the see of Rome before him, he was distracted by more pressing matters nearer home.

But the long-sought-after liberating Crusades were never revived. Attack and counterattack seemed to be over. For a little while at least.

The Tides of Time

Because *Ji'had* is an innate aspect of Islam, Muslims have never abandoned the ambition to conquer the world and subjugate the infidels. From time to time they experience revival and launch a new initiative.

At the beginning of the sixteenth century, the Ottoman Sultan Selim called for a renewed *Ji'had* and added Greece, Macedonia, and the Balkans to his empire. His son, Suleiman, swept into Belgrade in 1521, expelled the Templars from Rhodes in 1522, and conquered Hungary in 1526. Then in 1529 he entered the very heart of Christian Europe, ready to crush the church once and for all. According to one of his chroniclers at the time, he confidently boasted, "The infidels will at last bow in submission to Allah. The time for judgment has come just as their prophets have said. The *Ji'had* has advanced its full course and the end is now in sight. The abomination of the Christian heresy shall be no more."[8]

His siege of Vienna that winter was, in a very real sense, Europe's last stand. If he had prevailed there, no army of any significance

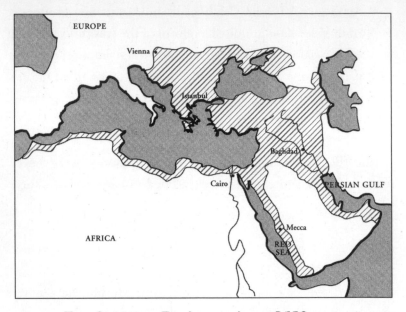

The Ottoman Empire, circa 1530 A.D.

would have been able to stop him until he reached the outskirts of Paris. But because of a valiant and united defense, he did not prevail, and Christendom was saved.

After Suleiman passed from the scene, calls for *Ji'had* came only sporadically—during times of Islamic revival or at revolutionary flash points. The Ottoman Empire drifted into a mediocre stasis. And the West began to forget about its Eastern nemesis while it rushed headlong into cosmopolitan modernity.

The resurgence of Arab nationalistic fervor that followed World War II in Egypt and Syria under the leadership of Gamal Abdel Nasser was a short-lived attempt to reestablish the hegemony of Saladin or Suleiman on a secular foundation. But its momentum simply could not outlast the charismatic leader who first gave it impetus. When he died, it died.

And then came the Ayatollah Khomeini and the frightening specter of his Islamic fundamentalism, which was really nothing more than a return to historic and orthodox Koranic Islam.

His sudden overthrow of the shah in Iran in 1979 renewed the international call for *Ji'had*. Shortly after installing his revolutionary government in Tehran, the Ayatollah asserted, "We shall export our revolution to the whole world. Until the cry '*Allah Akbar*' resounds over the whole world, there will be struggle. There will be *Ji'had*."[9]

He continued,

> Islam is the religion of militant individuals who are committed to truth and justice. It is the religion of those who desire freedom and independence. It is the school of those who struggle against imperialism. Weapons in our hands are used to realize divine and Islamic aspirations. The more people who die for our cause, the stronger our *Ji'had* shall become.[10]

His plea was explicit: faithful Muslims were to wreak havoc the world over in the name of Allah. Western nations were to be overthrown. Any option open and available should be exercised for the sake of Islam, from terrorism to revolution, from subversion to full-scale war: "The governments of the world should know that Islam cannot be defeated. Islam will be victorious in all the countries of the world, and Islam and the teachings of the Koran will prevail all over the world."[11]

Therefore, he declared,

> We have in reality, then, no choice but to destroy those systems of government that are corrupt in themselves and also entail the

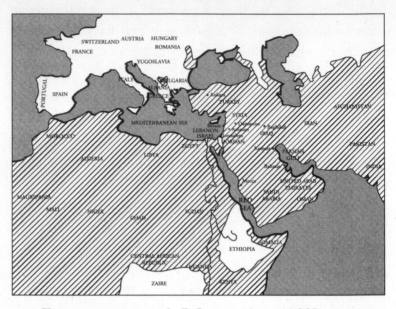

The conquests of Islam, circa 2001 A.D.

corruption of others, and to overthrow all treacherous, corrupt, oppressive, and criminal regimes. This is the duty that all Muslims must fulfill, in every one of the Muslim countries first, and then throughout the infidel West, in order to achieve the triumph of our revolution and to garner the blessing of Allah.[12]

There would be—in fact, there could be—no compromise. The die was cast. The stage was set.

The recent spate of terrorism—hijackings, bombings, kidnappings, attacks, and even direct military confrontations—that has been inflicted upon the West is clear testimony to the fact that Islam's *Ji'had* is anything but a forgotten relic of the past.

During the days of mobilization for World War I, when it looked for a time that American troops would be deployed in the

Middle East against the fierce Ottomans, a young Presbyterian pastor, James Alexander Bryan, eloquently expressed the key message of the ages:

> Let all be done bathed in prayer—our working and our playing, our eating and our sleeping, our dreaming and our doing. Let all be done bathed in prayer. But most particularly, when we know that our boys, our sons, and our brothers, and our husbands, must face those denizens of terror from the desert realms of the Levant, should we bathe our very inner being, our breathing, and our thinking in prayer. Dost thou not know that the hosts of Cain and the minions of Babel, the legions of Saracene and the hordes of Arabia are set from eternity against the covenant people. Pray therefore. Night and day, pray. Moment by moment, pray. Pray for mercy. O dear souls, pray.[13]

Pray because the passion for *Ji'had* will not go away simply because we deploy troops in impressive and deadly array. Pray because the desire for *Dhimmi* will continue to divide East and West despite our carefully constructed international coalitions and strategic alliances. Pray because it's never over till it's over.

Chapter Seven

A Peace to End All Peace

We must diligently strive to make our young men decent,
God-fearing, law-abiding, honor-loving, justice-doing, and
also fearless and strong, able to hold their own in the hurly-
burly of the world's work, able to strive mightily that the forces
of right may be in the end triumphant. And we must be ever
vigilant in so telling them.

—THEODORE ROOSEVELT[1]

At one time, Beirut was known the world over as the jewel of
the Mediterranean. With its spectacular beaches, its splendid
hotels, and its moderate climate, it had become the playground
of the jet set and the most desirable destination in the entire
Middle East. But those days are now long gone. Beirut is little
more than a bombed-out shell. It is a trash-strewn, rubble-filled,
grief-stricken battlefield where the acrimonious ambitions of the
region have overtaken its everyday life and brought to ruin its
civilization.

In 1983, President Ronald Reagan sent a large contingent of
crack American troops, including an entire marine battalion, to
that war-torn city as part of the U.N. Multinational Peacekeeping
Force. He hoped their presence would help bring an end to the

bitter civil war that had divided Lebanon's Christian and Muslim populations since at least 1975.

On the morning of October 23, a large cargo truck loaded with explosives made its way into Beirut's international airport toward the marine command center. As the suicide bomber crashed his truck into the building, he was heard screaming his final message to the world: "Allah Akbar! Ji'had! Ji'had! Ji'had!" Moments later, rescuers began frantically digging through the rubble of twisted steel and crumpled concrete searching for survivors. Instead, they found 241 Americans dead and scores more disabled for life. In an anonymous telephone call after the attack, a group calling itself the Islamic Ji'had claimed responsibility for the attack and promised many more to come.

Less than six months later, the president gave up his hopes for peace in the region and ordered the remaining troops home.

They returned gladly.

Because the Middle East has been the battleground for men's passions since the beginning of time, virtually every scheme imaginable has been attempted in the hope that one day real and lasting peace might be attained. Invariably whenever the West has assumed the role of peacemaker, conquest, colonialism, containment, or appeasement has been at the heart of its scheme. And just as invariably such mechanistic and materialistic methodologies fall short of the mark of peace.

Conquest

In 1796, a young Corsican military commander for the French republic made a name for himself in a series of innovative land maneuvers that liberated all of Lombardy from the dominion of

Austria. Well-educated, properly connected, and insanely ambitious, Napoleon Bonaparte effulgently guided his motley legions against the infinitely larger and better-equipped armies of the Habsburgs, the Hohenzollerns, the Wettins, the Wittelsbachs, and the Oldenburgs. He swept aside their superiority in battle after battle with unconventional ripostes and ambushes. His achievements were nothing short of brilliant.

But it seems his ego was at least as great as his achievements were. By the time he had established republican rule in Venice, Milan, and Genoa, he had already begun to imagine himself an imperial conqueror. He styled himself a Caesar.

He returned to Paris a hero. The city, weary and worn from the long traumas of revolutionary anarchy, was anxious for some beacon of hope. From the people in the streets to the nobles in the salons, Napoleon represented that hope. He was successful. He was undefeatable. And he was irrepressible.

So confident was the government in his abilities that the Directorate urged him in 1797 to assume leadership of all the French armed forces and lead an expedition, first to pacify England, and then to pacify the world.

Thinking more like a Roman Caesar or a Greek Alexander than a modern European general, he redirected their focus:

> The key to containing the English and to bringing peace to the world is not to attack England. It is to capture the Levant and control all its commerce with India and the East. Peace has always turned upon Alexandria, Jerusalem, Acre, and Constantinople. It always will. Control them and you can control the world. Bring them peace and you bring peace to the world.[2]

And so the French Caesar set out to wage his peace.

Eluding the English fleet in the Mediterranean, his forces crossed from Malta to the mouth of the Nile and quickly occupied the great old city of Alexandria. The meager Turkish defenses surrendered. Shortly thereafter, Aboukir and Cairo also capitulated. Although his naval support was no match for the English flotilla, he confidently moved out from under its cover and on to Jaffa and Acre.

His plan was to secure Egypt, Syria, Palestine, and ultimately the entire Middle East as a platform to launch a series of world-wide conquests. It was to be the first prize in a far-flung French empire—the beginning of a glorious new Pax Française.

But all did not work out as planned.

First, Admiral Nelson captured the vulnerable French fleet in the Aboukir Bay, cutting Napoleon off from reinforcements and supplies. Then, the Turkish defenders at Acre retreated into the old Crusader battlements where they could not be flushed out. And then, ethnic and tribal disputes nullified any advantage that he might have gained from the diplomatic alliance that he had forged with indigenous Arab sultanates.

In 1799, Napoleon gave up and fled the region. Although he had the overwhelming advantage over his foes—he had by far the finest fighting force, the most brilliant strategy, and the clearest vision—he was soundly defeated. His dream of peace in the region eluded him.

Of course, Napoleon would quickly recover from that first defeat and rise to unimagined heights. But he would never forget his difficult foray into peacemaking-by-conquest in the Middle East. He wrote from St. Helena at the end of his life:

Of all the defeats that I have tasted none has been so bitter—not even Waterloo—than my defeat at Acre. For it was there that Fate or Providence determined that I should never rule the world and that a French-directed peace would never prevail. I knew it then. I knew it ever afterward. No empire can ever be wrought without the peace of Jerusalem at its center because that is the hinge of history. But then, no empire can ever be wrought with the peace of Jerusalem at its center because such peace is humanly unattainable. It is an impossible mysterious mistress.[3]

Napoleon had to learn the lesson that would-be conquerors have been learning in the Middle East for centuries: sheer force or superior armaments or finely hewn strategies are not sufficient to bring peace to the region. It is a wild and unpredictable land where swirling spiritual obsessions and disparate human passions compete on an even keel with steadfast reason and cold pragmatism.

Napoleon had to learn that the hard way.

Colonialism

The accession of the Christian culture of Europe as the world's dominating sociopolitical force was not assured until well into the nineteenth century. For the bulk of its first two millennia Christian culture had been strikingly unsuccessful in spreading its beneficent effects beyond European shores. In the Far East, missionary endeavors were practically nonexistent in China and paralyzed by persecution in Japan. In India, the higher castes were virtually untouched by the gospel, and even the lower castes showed only transitory interest. South America's conversion to the conquistadors' Catholicism was tenuous at best. And tropical Africa had proved to be so formidable and inhospitable that Western settlements were confined to a few small outposts along the coast. Ever since the Middle East had been lost to Islam, Christianity had become little more than a regional phenomenon.

There had been a few bursts of expansion beginning in the sixteenth century. Explorers tentatively ventured out into uncharted realms. Scientists began to probe long-hidden mysteries. Traders and merchants carved out new routes, new markets, and new technologies. Energies that had previously been devoted exclusively to survival were redirected by local magistrates into projects and programs designed to improve health, hygiene, and the common good. Africa, India, China, Indonesia, and the Americas were opened to exploration and exploitation. From colonial outposts there, a tremendous wealth of exotic raw resources poured into European cities.

Despite all these advantages, however, European advances were limited and short-lived. Internecine warfare and petty territorialism disrupted, and very nearly nullified, even that much Christian influence. From 1688 (when William and Mary concluded the Glorious Revolution in England by ascending to the throne, Louis XIV canonized the iron-fisted notion of divine right, and young Peter Romanov became czar of all the Russias) until 1848—when the calamitous Marxist rebellions in Paris, Rome, Venice, Berlin, Parma, Vienna, and Milan were finally squelched—one convulsive struggle after another racked Europe.

But then, almost suddenly, everything changed.

Three great revolutions, beginning first in England and then spreading throughout all the European dominions, laid the foundations for this turn of events.

The first was the Agricultural Revolution. The replacement of fallowing with leguminous rotation, the use of chemical fertilizers, and the introduction of farm machinery enabled Europeans to virtually break the cycle of famine and triage across the continent for the first time in mankind's history.

The second was the Industrial Revolution. Manufactured goods and the division of labor created a broad-based middle class and freed the unlanded masses—again, for the first time in human history.

The third was the Transportation Revolution. At the beginning of the nineteenth century, Napoleon could not cross his domain any more efficiently than Nebuchadnezzar could have six centuries before Christ. By the end of the Victorian age, men were racing across the rails and roads in motorized vehicles of stupendous power, crashing over and under the waves of the sea in iron vessels of enormous size, and cutting through the clouds in ingenious zeppelins, balloons, and planes.

Within a single generation, the earth became a European planet. Whole continents were carved up between competing monarchs. Africa, Asia, Australia, the Far East, Latin America, and even the Middle East became the backyard playgrounds of speculative colonialists and imperial opportunists.

England differed from its rivals in that it had somehow come to realize that peace could not be won by naked conquest alone. It attempted to exact peace through colonization. The beachhead for the British in foreign lands was trade, not war. Instead of sending armies, they sent merchants. Not surprisingly the merchants were less threatening than the armies and were more often than not very well received. As a result, the empire of Queen Victoria grew at a phenomenal rate and became mind-bogglingly prosperous. In Africa, India, and the Far East, English businessmen established an economic commonwealth that only gradually became a full-fledged political empire.

In the Middle East, the same kind of colonial philanthropy enabled Britain to step into the void left by the dismantled Ottoman Empire after World War I. But it was in for a rude awakening.

Unprepared for the roiling passions that divided various Muslim factions, the bitter acrimony between the Jews and their neighbors, and the pitiful rivalry of innumerable tribal and ethnic legions, the English peacemakers found themselves on the horns of an awful dilemma. For several decades they tried to extricate themselves from what their diplomats called the Eastern Question—all to no avail:

- In 1916, they concluded the Sikes-Picot negotiations with France, thus denying the possibility of Arab hegemony.

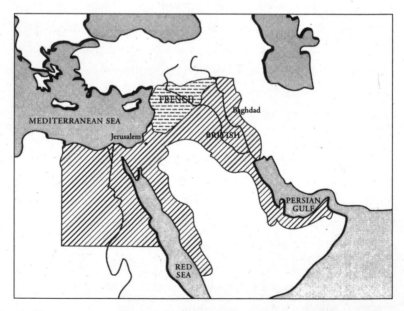

European colonial domains, circa 1918 A.D.

- In 1917, they issued the Balfour Declaration, pledging to secure the establishment of a Jewish Palestinian state.

- The next year, 1918, they accepted and endorsed Woodrow Wilson's Fourteen Points as a basis for cessation of hostilities in World War I, including the guarantee of autonomy for the Arabs as a precondition for the armistice.

- In 1919, they embraced the Hashemite Emir Faisal's Plan for Arab National Unity presented to the Supreme Council at the Paris Peace Conference.

- In 1920, they accepted the National Pact presented by the Ottoman Chamber of Deputies, thus permanently dividing the old Syrian districts.

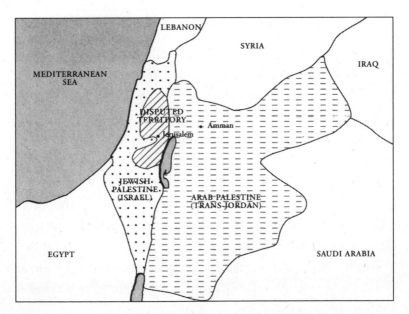

The partitioning of Palestine, circa 1948 A.D.

- In 1921, they offered the Hashemite, Abdullah, free sovereignty in Trans-Jordan and exemption from the Balfour Declaration.

- In 1922, they released a statement of British Policy on Palestine, responding to both Arab and Zionist pressures by establishing the Hashemite regencies in Iraq, Hejaz, Syria, and Palestine.

- In 1925, they approved the ouster of the Hashemite, Sharif Hussein, from Mecca, and the subsequent absorption of Hejaz into the Saudi kingdom.

- In 1928, they finalized a treaty with Trans-Jordan and Iraq, enraging the Zionists due to its betrayal of the conditions of Balfour.

- In 1937, they severely restricted Jewish immigration to Palestine with the Ridenour Policy, thus stranding hundreds of dispossessed souls on the island of Cyprus.

- And in 1946, they attempted to partition Palestine into Arab and Jewish regions—a plan endorsed by the United Nations and partially implemented in 1948.

The problem with these painfully negotiated policies, concords, treaties, pacts, alliances, and settlements was that virtually every one of them contradicted all the others. The colonizing principle that seemed to work so well in other parts of the world, ushering in an age of Pax Britannia, failed miserably in the complex and discrepant Middle East.

Finally, in frustration, the British peacemakers pulled out in 1948. Their only other foray into the region ended in disaster in 1956 at the Suez Canal.

Like Napoleon, they had to learn the hard way.

Containment

Ever since the imperial armies had secured the southern territories along the Black Sea in 1558, the great czars who successively ruled the vast dominions of Russia coveted a warm-water port— a trade outlet to the Mediterranean. In addition, they believed that a forcible containment of the Islamic threat to their strategic security was absolutely crucial. As a result, over the last five hundred years Russia has fought more wars in the Middle East than any other nation on earth.

It engaged the Ottoman Turks seven different times over a period of three hundred years—in 1568–1569, in 1678–1681, in 1697–1700, in 1710–11, in 1736–39, in 1828–29, and in 1877–78. It engaged Persia four times over a period of two hundred years—in 1722–23, in 1804–13, in 1906–9, and in 1911–12. And it has engaged Afghanistan three times over a period of one hundred years—in 1885–86, in 1941–43, and in 1979–89.

None of those struggles resulted in much change in the balance of power in the Middle East, and Russia was continually rebuffed in the region. The rest of the world paid little attention. But then, between 1853 and 1856, the Russian policy of containment brought the Russians to the brink of world war in the Crimea.

In a jurisdictional dispute over the holy places of Ottoman-controlled Jerusalem, Czar Nicholas I finally determined to protect and enforce the interests of Christians within the Turkish Empire's territories. The Ottoman emissaries in Russia were outraged at the czar's audacity and spurned all his attempts to communicate directly with the sultan. In frustration, Nicholas ordered his forces to occupy Turkish Moldavia, Serbia, and Wallachia. The Ottomans quickly declared war.

Fearful of Russian intentions, France, Britain, Austria, Sardinia, and Prussia all signed defensive pacts with the Turks. In addition, thousands of Bedouins and Arab merchants volunteered to beat the Russian "infidels" away from their borders. A short time later, when a Russian naval squadron bombarded and destroyed an Ottoman flotilla at Sinop, the new international alliance of Europeans and Arabs moved into the area and launched a bloody and protracted war. After the Battle of Balaklava—immortalized in Tennyson's famous poem *The Charge of the Light Brigade*— Russian troops were forced into retreat, and the czar was compelled to sue for peace.

Like the French and the British, he failed to recognize the conflux of spiritual passions and geopolitical jealousies that make containment—or any other mere material policy—in the Middle East utterly hopeless.

Appeasement

Modern historians have dubbed the past hundred years "the American Century" and for good reason. America's transformation from a provincial and isolated republican experiment in the nineteenth century to an international superpower in the twentieth is one of the most stunning events in human memory.

Like the French, the British, and the Russians, Americans have sought to wield their influence around the globe in order to encourage freedom and to establish peace. But they have done it while repudiating conquest, colonialism, and containment. Rather than trying to occupy or balkanize regions, the United States has sought merely to influence. It has sought to leverage competing concerns and balance intractable conflicts. It has taken the course of appeasement.

At first blush, the strategy appeared to be a good one: use the leverage of foreign aid and strategic cooperation to win friends and influence enemies, to stymie the advances of the Soviet Union, and to open new markets for American products and investment.

Practically, though, the result of this foreign policy, particularly in the Middle East, has produced scant improvement over our Western predecessors' efforts. It has often led us to fund both sides of a conflict—building simultaneously the Israeli and the Arab military capabilities—on the pretense that a balance of power serves as the best hedge against communism. It has often led us to betray our proved friends and support our sworn enemies—allowing the Phalangist and Maronite Christians under the leadership of General Aoun to be massacred by Hafez al Assad's Hezbollah Syrian troops in Lebanon—on the pretense that stability in the region required the sacrifice of certain interests. And it has led us to befriend despots and defend tyrannies—allying ourselves with Saudi Arabia and Kuwait, where slavery and indentured servitude are still practiced—on the pretense that international pluralism must make room for cultural diversity. Far from securing American interests and concerns, this kind of philosophical and moral schizophrenia has led us into one dead end after another.

Consider the remarkable record of American appeasement with Saddam Hussein and Iraq:

- When Iraqi Exocet missiles killed thirty-seven United States seamen aboard the *USS Stark* in 1987, the State Department blamed Iran and excused our ally Saddam altogether.

- When Iraq used chemical weapons in a genocidal attack on its own Kurdish citizens in 1988, our government turned a blind eye.

- Even after Saddam established Baghdad as a haven for international terrorists—including Abul Abass, the hijacker of the *Achille Lauro*—we removed Iraq from our list of terrorist states.

- In 1989, the U.S. refused to join twelve other Western nations calling for a United Nations inquiry into Iraqi human rights violations.

- In 1990, our government failed to protest the forcible relocation of more than half a million Kurds and Syrians in Iraq.

- The State Department successfully fought against the legislative efforts of Senators Jesse Helms, Caliborne Pell, and Al D'Amato to impose sanctions on Iraq and its suppliers.

- Between 1982 and 1991 when the Gulf War broke out, we provided Iraq with more than $5 million of American products and taxpayer-guaranteed loans and subsidies.

- During the same time we secured nearly $300 million of credit for Saddam from the Export-Import Bank.

- Days before the invasion of Saddam's Persian Gulf neighbor, the United States ambassador to Iraq told Saddam that, since we had no defensive alliance with Kuwait, we saw the conflict between the two nations as a routine Arab border dispute.

- Though Iraq had invaded Kuwait twice previously and was threatening to do so again—voicing the same grievances each time, in 1961, in 1973, and again in 1990—our government had always deigned to remain neutral.

- On the very day before the invasion of Kuwait, State Department officials were on Capitol Hill lobbying for an increased financial aid package for Iraq.

- Yet one week later, Saddam was labeled as a Hitler and a madman who simply had to be stopped.

- The Gulf War was fought and won, after the U.S. mobilized a remarkable international coalition. Yet Saddam was not stopped. He was not deposed. And his reign of terror in the region was not ended.

- Though he refused to cooperate with United Nations weapons inspectors, though he continued his program of harassment against his own Kurdish population, though he continually threatened the security of the Kuwaiti borders, and though he sponsored and encouraged global terrorism, Saddam continued to hold on to the reins of power in Baghdad.

Like Napoleon's conquests, Britain's colonization, and Russia's containment, America's appeasement has failed to bring peace to the region. Because all approached the Middle East from a mechanistic and materialistic perspective—assuming that the imposition of Western notions of pluralism, economic development, and international cooperation are paramount values shared by all—they failed miserably to comprehend the complex maze of spiritual and historical factors that catalyzes the crisis in the Middle East.

We, too, have had to learn that lesson the hard way.

True Peace

The prophet Isaiah brought a message to those who lived in the Middle East thousands of years ago. That message is as relevant today as when he first uttered it:

> "Peace, peace to him who is far and to him who is near,"
> Says the LORD, "and I will heal him."
> But the wicked are like the tossing sea,
> For it cannot be quiet,
> And its waters toss up refuse and mud.
> "There is no peace," says my God, "for the wicked."
>   (Isa. 57:19–21)

With remarkable economy and startling clarity, that message traverses both space and time to bring into focus the complex dilemma of spreading peace throughout our strife-riven world.

Isaiah had dedicated his life to proclaiming God's eternal purposes for mankind. He was a diligent bearer of the glad tidings of peace. After all, God had established a covenant of peace with His people (Isa. 54:10). It was an irrevocable and everlasting covenant (Isa. 61:8). Thus, they had the promise of peace with the nations around them and with God Himself (Isa. 26:12; 27:5). They would have peace "like a river" (Isa. 66:12) and peace "like the waves of the sea" (Isa. 48:18). It would be a perfect peace wrought by the Prince of Peace (Isa. 9:6; 26:3).

This remarkable promise of peace was indeed good news and glad tidings. But Isaiah made it abundantly apparent that the promise could be redeemed only by the righteous. Peace on earth and goodwill toward men are available only to those on whom God's favor rests (Luke 2:14 NIV). No peace, much less this promised utopian peace, will ever be attained by use of sheer force of aggression. No peace will ever be attained by mere appeasement or compromise. No peace will ever be attained by clever negotiation or wily manipulation. Nothing could be clearer: "There is no peace for the wicked" (Isa. 48:22). There never has been, and there never will be.

Things just aren't always as they seem. That is the dilemma of living in a fallen world. G. K. Chesterton brilliantly captured the essence of this dilemma when he wrote:

> The real trouble with this world of ours is not that it is an unreasonable world, nor even that it is a reasonable one. The commonest kind of trouble is that it is nearly reasonable, but not quite. Life is not an illogicality; yet it is a trap for logicians. It looks just a little more mathematical and regular than it is; its exactitude is obvious, but its inexactitude is hidden; its wildness lies in wait . . . It is this silent swerving from accuracy by an inch that is the uncanny element in everything. It seems a sort of secret treason in the universe. An apple or an orange is round enough to get itself called round, and yet is not round after all. The earth itself is shaped like an orange in order to lure some simple astronomer into calling it a globe. A blade of grass is called after a blade of the sword, because it comes to a point; but it doesn't. Everywhere in things there is this element of the quiet and incalculable.[4]

Mirroring the world's fallenness, the uncanny element in the efforts of the West to achieve peace in the Middle East is its silent swerving from accuracy by an inch. Its exactitude is obvious, but its inexactitude is hidden; its wildness lies in wait. It is almost operatic in its unreality, creating a peace to end all peace.

Things just aren't always as they seem.

Even so, God has called us to peace (1 Cor. 7:15). He has called us to be peacemakers (Matt. 5:9). If we genuinely desire a true peace, a lasting peace, and a just peace, then we have only one course to follow—the course of righteousness. Therefore, let us "pursue the things which make for peace" (Rom. 14:19).

Part Three

The Future and Faith

Nothing is more unbecoming than sullenly to gnaw the bit with which we are bridled, and to withhold our groaning from God, if indeed we have any faith in His promise.

—JOHN CALVIN[1]

I charge you therefore before God and the Lord Jesus Christ, who will judge the living and the dead at His appearing and His kingdom: Preach the word! Be ready in season and out of season. Convince, rebuke, exhort, with all longsuffering and teaching. For the time will come when they will not endure sound doctrine, but according to their own desires, because they have itching ears, they will heap up for themselves teachers; and they will turn their ears away from the truth, and be turned aside to fables.

—2 TIMOTHY 4:1–4 NKJV

Chapter Eight

Back to Babel

What we demand is nothing peculiar to ourselves. It is that the world be made fit and safe to live in, and particularly that it be made safe for every peace-loving nation which, like our own, wishes to live its own life, determine its own institutions, be assured of justice and fair dealing by the other peoples of the world as against force and selfish aggression. For our own part, we see very clearly that unless justice be done to others it will not be done to us. The program of the world's peace, therefore, is our program.

—Woodrow Wilson[1]

Men are forever attempting to remake their world—to usher in a new utopian age of infinite justice, enduring freedom, and perpetual peace. They are constantly attempting to create a kind of new world order.

During the last century, that ambition became something like an obsession. A kind of secularized millennial vision drove men and nations to disrupt and disturb long-settled human institutions—all in an effort to forge a new pathway to some new and improved future. This disastrous peculiarity of modernism was the fruit of a strange innovation in the affairs of men. According to Paul Johnson, "With the decline of clerical power in the nine-teenth century, a new kind of mentor emerged to fill the vacuum and capture the ear of society. The secular intellectual might be deist, skeptic, or atheist. But he was just as ready as any pontiff, presbyter, or imam to tell mankind how to conduct its affairs."[2]

This new breed of prophet, priest, and king brought a tragic compulsion to his task of remaking the world in which he lived:

> He proclaimed from the start, a special devotion to the interests of humanity and an evangelical duty to advance them by his teaching. He brought to this self-appointed task a far more radical approach than his clerical predecessors. He felt himself bound by no corpus of revealed religion. The collective wisdom of the past, the legacy of tradition, the prescriptive codes of ancestral experience existed to be selectively followed or wholly rejected entirely as his own good sense might decide. For the first time in human history, and with growing confidence and audacity, men arose to assert that they could diagnose the ills of society and cure them with their own unaided intellects: more, that they could devise formulae whereby not merely the structure of society but the fundamental habits of human beings could be transformed for the better. Unlike their sacerdotal predecessors, they were not servants and interpreters of the gods but substitutes. Their hero was Prometheus, who stole celestial fire and brought it to earth.[3]

As a result, this motley band of social engineers marshaled little more than their wits in their attempts at reinventing mankind—a task no less arduous and no less ludicrous than reinventing the wheel. The result was predictably deleterious.

Ultimately the new world order of these wild-eyed secular

idealists was dashed against the hard reality of history. The sad experience of the twentieth century—two devastating world wars, unnumbered holocausts and genocides, the fierce tyrannies of communism's evil empire, violent nationalist movements built on foundations of terror and repression, and the embarrassing foibles of liberalism's welfare state—exposed its high-flying ideals as the noisome eccentricities that they are.

Again and again the story that history has told during the last two centuries is the story of the folly of expert and meticulous men attempting to reengineer society in accord with their own preferences, redraw the maps of the world according to their own peculiar design, realign ancient passions by means of their own modern mechanics, and resolve spiritual dilemmas by means of their own temporal values. The result has been nothing less than a designer disaster.

Despite history's stern rebuke, though, there are still a few die-hard devotees of this ever-hopeful worldview at work in our society—many of them are even now at work attempting to resolve the historic conflict between Islam and Western civilization. Their cant is rather ragged and shop-worn, but their influence has not yet altogether disappeared. According to historian William Gairdner, they are intent on making one last-ditch effort to usher in their glorious world vision:

> The legions of well-intentioned but smug, educated elites have agreed in advance to reject thousands of years of inherited wisdom, values, habit, custom, and insight and replace this heritage with their official utopian vision of the perfect society. They are the progressives, and they can be found in every political party. Trained as scientific, or logical rationalists, these social utopians haughtily

treat all social or moral traditions and conventions as arbitrary, rather than as venerable repositories of indispensable social, family, and religious values. They despise natural authority, especially of a local or family variety, and they want to replace it with a sufficiently homogenous state power to bring about their coercive social dreamland. So with a government wage or grant in one hand and a policy whip in the other, they set about forcibly aligning individuals and customs with their dangerously narrow vision, then clamor after ever greater funding and ever more progressive legislation for the education or socialization of the people.[4]

Despite their best efforts, they will fail, of course—just as they always have in the past. The Middle East is hardly the sort of place where experimental policies are apt to find success. The efficacy of their policies and programs aside, every megatrend evidenced in our society today bodes ill for them: the restoration of accountability, thrift, decentralization, and independence in civic affairs; the return to lasting values, personal responsibility, substantive virtues, and enduring tradition in private affairs; and the reaffirmation of beauty, integrity, edification, and inspiration in cultural affairs. Though they may yet wreak havoc on our families, our communities, and our freedoms, the social engineers ultimately will go the way of the ray gun, the zeppelin dock, and the electromagneto aerial car.

Science is not infallible. Society is not perfectible. Utopia is not attainable. All the money, all the educational programs, all the technological breakthroughs, all the diplomatic ingenuity, and all the compulsion our philosopher-kings can muster cannot make it so. There is one fact that contravenes their fondest hopes and most fantastic dreams. It is the one fact that their steely-eyed, new world order bureaucrats never reckoned with.

It is the fact of the Fall.

If Islam's great flaw is an inadequate view of the Fall, perhaps it is a flaw it shares with much of the West in thrall to Modernity.

The Tower of Power

According to the Bible, the first concerted effort to establish a new world order came at Babel:

> Now the whole earth used the same language and the same words. And it came about as they journeyed east, that they found a plain in the land of Shinar and settled there. And they said to one another, "Come, let us make bricks and burn them thoroughly." And they used brick for stone, and they used tar for mortar. And they said, "Come, let us build for ourselves a city, and a tower whose top will reach into heaven, and let us make for ourselves a name; lest we be scattered abroad over the face of the whole earth." (Gen. 11:1–4)

Apparently the goal of Nimrod and the other members of his seventy-nation alliance (Gen. 10:2–32) was to establish the global enforcement of at least five major objectives:

First, they desired to preserve some sort of universal cultural consensus, or worldwide ideological communion, among the nations. The biblical account asserts that "the whole earth used the same language and the same words" (Gen. 11:1). It wasn't just that all of the nations spoke the same language. It was that they spoke the same language because they were bound by the same culture. They were of one mind. They shared a common philosophical outlook. They had the same worldview. Babel, then, was an attempt to institutionalize that unity so that it might be adequately preserved.

Second, the leaders of the international coalition at Babel wanted to impose increasing secularization on human society. According to the narrative, these events occurred as the nations "journeyed east" (Gen. 11:2). Throughout the Bible, eastward migrations are invariably associated with rebellion against the will and purpose of God. The word *nasa,* translated "journeyed" here, literally means to "pull out" or "abandon." When Adam and Eve abandoned Eden, they journeyed east (Gen. 3:24). After Cain killed his brother, Abel, he abandoned his home and journeyed east (Gen. 4:16). When Lot abandoned Abraham to seek his fortunes in the lush valley of Sodom, he journeyed east (Gen. 13:11). Again and again the pattern is reinforced in Scripture: moving east is symbolic of abandoning righteousness. Babel, then, was a very straightforward rebellion against God's standards of morality and ethics in society.

Third, the organizers of the Babel debacle wanted to secure their base of power. The biblical account says that they set to work building "a tower whose top will reach into heaven" (Gen. 11:4). Of course, they knew that they could not build an architectural structure that would pierce the atmosphere and intrude into the heavenly realm. A tower in the ancient world was a kind of artificial mountain sanctuary where men could grasp the power of the Divine. The Garden of Eden was on a mountain (Ezek. 28:13–14). But ever since the Fall, when men were denied access to that sanctuary, they had sought appropriate alternatives because they were not satisfied with the alternative that God Himself had provided (Gen. 3:16–26). Having been barred from the presence of God, they aspired to literally storm the gates of His habitation by building a kind of stairway to heaven. They were trying to steal holy fire. They were trying to secure the blessing, and perhaps even the power, of God on their own terms and by their own strength. Babel was simply a humanistic power play. It was a ploy designed to "end run" God's providence.

Fourth, the perpetrators of the Babel incident sought to establish their autonomy and self-determination. The narrative says that they wanted to make a name for themselves. Throughout the Bible, naming is an important activity. A person's name defined his character. If a person's character altered significantly sometime during his life, his name would be altered as well. Thus, whenever anyone was converted, his name was changed. For instance, Abram was changed to Abraham, Sarai to Sarah, Jacob to Israel, Simon to Peter, and Saul to Paul. In every case, a parent or God Himself did the naming. But the leaders of the seventy-nation alliance at Babel determined that they would short-circuit that divine prerogative and make a name for themselves. Babel, then, was a declaration of independence from God. It was an act of prideful, humanistic rebellion.

Fifth, the pioneers of the new world order at Babel attempted to centralize control over every aspect of the social structure. The Genesis account says that they were fearful of being "scattered abroad over the face of the whole earth" (11:4). The only reason that they were frightened of that was that God had told them to scatter. They were frightened of obedience to His will:

Be fruitful and multiply; fill the earth and subdue it; have dominion over the fish of the sea, over the birds of the air, and over every living thing that moves on the earth. (Gen. 1:28 NKJV)

Be fruitful and multiply, and fill the earth. And the fear of you and the dread of you shall be on every beast of the earth, on every bird of the air, on all that move on the earth, and on all the fish of the sea. They are given into your hand. (Gen. 9:1–2 NKJV)

Once again, the purpose of Babel was to subvert God's sovereign purposes for human society by institutionalizing an alternative, centralized authority structure: their own.

Though the effort was rather ingenious, the great experiment on the plain of Shinar failed miserably—as all attempts to mechanically establish a new world order eventually do:

> The LORD came down to see the city and the tower which the sons of men had built. And the LORD said, "Indeed the people are one and they all have one language, and this is what they begin to do; now nothing that they propose to do will be withheld from them. Come, let Us go down and there confuse their language, that they may not understand one another's speech." So the LORD scattered them abroad from there over the face of all the earth, and they ceased building the city. Therefore its name is called Babel, because there the LORD confused the language of all the earth; and from there the LORD scattered them abroad over the face of all the earth. (Gen. 11:5–9 NKJV)

The alliance was broken. The universal creed was confused. The tower was deserted. And the new world order was thrown into disarray. For a time.

The Empire Impulse

G. K. Chesterton warned that we should always

> beware of men and of movements that speak the language of Babel. Regardless of whether they are Communists or Fascists, Universalists or Deists, Socialists or Capitalists, Alchemists or

Templars, Liberals or Conservatives: beware of their New World
Order; beware of their Peace In Our Time; beware of their New
Age; beware of their Fraternal Harmony; beware of their Novus
Ordo Saeculorum. It is merely part and parcel of that same Tower
of Babel impulse which God cursed so long ago. It is merely a new
sprig from the primordial root of humanism: man seizing his own
destiny and making a name for himself in the annals of history.[5]

Just as the attraction of empire building has always plagued
mankind, the language of Babel continues to be the common
currency of modern diplomacy. In fact, virtually all of the most
influential voices in the international community are using the
same language and the same words. They all cry out for the global
establishment of the principles of Babel—hegemony, secularism,
power, autonomy, and centralization—over and above any other
concerns. The empire impulse is still very much alive.

The United Nations, for instance, was founded in 1945 as
"man's last hope for peace." But its interest in peace has been
terribly selective through the years. Instead, it has steadfastly lob-
bied for the principles of Babel. When the Soviet Union invaded
Hungary in 1956, Czechoslovakia in 1968, and Afghanistan in
1979, the United Nations Security Council uttered nary a peep.
Somehow, it also overlooked the blandishments of genocide in
Cambodia in 1975, the stench of triage in Ethiopia in 1984, and
the legions of international terrorism in Libya in 1986. When
hundreds of Christian Maronites were captured, bound, lined up,
and slaughtered in the streets of Lebanon in 1990 by the Syrian
army, the United Nations did not even take notice. After all, Syria
had become a "partner for peace" in the Middle East and a "strategic ally" in making the United Nations' new world order a reality.

Anything and everything, anyone and everyone, is expendable for the sake of Babel. The goal of achieving real peace is continually subverted to serve other ends—the ends of globalism and internationalism. As historian Paul Johnson asserted, "The United Nations had become a corrupt and demoralizing body, and its ill-considered actions were more inclined to promote violence than to prevent it."[6]

Because the United Nations had been so fitfully jockeying for the new world order, it did not have time to play the pipes of peace. Because it was so busy establishing and subsidizing the various organs of international centralization—the World Economic Community, the World Health Organization, the World Food and Energy Council, the World Bank, the World Council of Interdependence, and the World Affairs Council—it has ignored the globe's hottest hot spots. Because virtually every powerful internationalist institution—the Council on Foreign Relations, the Trilateral Commission, the Royal Institute for International Affairs, the Skull and Bones Club, and the Aspen Institute—recognizes the United Nations as the perfect forum for the implementation of its desperate Babel objectives, genuine peace has been shunted off the agenda.

When the crisis in the Middle East was inflamed once again during the Gulf War, the advocates of the new world order saw an opportunity to realize their designs at long last. That proved to be a rather ominous prospect, which has led to a decade of unfettered terrorism.

We would do well to heed the warning of Jesus:

Which of you, intending to build a tower, does not sit down first and count the cost, whether he has enough to finish it—lest, after he has laid the foundation, and is not able to finish it, all who see it begin to mock him, saying, "This man began to build and was not able to finish." Or what king, going to make war against another king, does not sit down first and consider whether he is able with ten thousand to meet him who comes against him with twenty thousand? Or else, while the other is still a great way off, he sends a delegation and asks conditions of peace. (Luke 14:28–32 NKJV)

The End Times

Many people fear that the road to a new world order is fraught with danger, and that it is quite literally the road to ruin. They believe that the chronology of recent events in the great East-West conflict is a countdown to Armageddon. They assert that the current crisis is pregnant with eschatological importance.

There are many others who see little, if any, prophetic significance.

The fact is, throughout the history of the church, there has been a great deal of diversity on the question of eschatology. Thus, through the centuries, faithful believers have differed greatly on the question of prophecy—and continue to do so.

Those who believe that prophecy is being fulfilled before our very eyes today cite the transformation of Eastern Europe, the crisis in Iraq, the isolation of Israel, and the solidifying of the European Economic Community as specific signs that we are now living in the last days. Wars and rumors of wars, famines, plagues, earthquakes, and pestilence—which all seem to be increasing in frequency and intensity—demonstrate beyond any shadow of a doubt that we have at last arrived at the end times.

In the Olivet Discourse—recorded in the gospel of Matthew—Jesus attempted to calm such speculative fears. He tried to show that eschatological pessimism is not consistent with faith in His kingdom.

Following His prediction that the temple in Jerusalem would soon be destroyed, His nervous disciples asked Him a series of questions: "When will these things be? And what will be the sign of Your coming, and of the end of the age?" (Matt. 24:3 NKJV).

Jesus responded by telling them that they had nothing to fear (Matt. 24:6). They were instead to be on guard against those who would unduly alarm and deceive them (Matt. 24:4). In spite of a spate of wars, rumors of wars, famines, pestilences, earthquakes, tribulations, and persecutions, they were to be assured that the end was not yet in sight (Matt. 24:6–12). He told them that those signs were just the beginnings of mankind's long and tortured struggle through history—the very birth pangs (Matt. 24:8). Instead of focusing on the subjective and often misleading signs of the times, Jesus directed their attention to the great task of preaching the gospel to all nations (Matt. 24:14).

Although His discourse is filled with specific portending prophecies—as the destruction of Jerusalem in A.D. 70 ultimately proved—the primary thrust of Christ's message was that eschatology is essentially ethical and only secondarily predictive. It is revealed by the good providence of God to provoke His people to uphold their responsibilities—to faithfully carry out the Great Commission, to diligently build up the church, to pray without ceasing, to engage in spiritual warfare, to serve the hurting and meet the needs of the innocent, to walk in holiness, and to live with one another in faith, hope, and love. In short, eschatology is a prod in the hands of God to incite the church to do right when all the rest of the world does wrong.

The new world order is no match, after all, for the empowered people of Christ Jesus. Scripture asserts, "His dominion is an everlasting dominion" (Dan. 4:34).

A Cosmic End Run

We usually think of the devil as an insidious destroyer. We are inclined to believe that his demonic plan has been, is now, and always will be to play fast and free with goodness, truth, and purity wherever they might be found, to possess individuals with destructive passions, to defile all honor, valor, and ethical seemliness.

The truth is, Satan does not so much want to tear down godly conventions and mores as to build up his own malevolent ones. He has always nurtured Babel-like aspirations to build a new world order and usher in a new age. He is always striving to make a name for himself and fill the world with his glory. In other words, it isn't that he wants to be a fiend; it is that he wants to be "like the Most High" (Isa. 14:14). His purpose has always been to build some glorious, utopian future of his own design—apart from God.

Otto Blumhardt, the pioneer Lutheran missionary to Africa in the seventeenth century, wrote,

> The devil's conceit is merely that he might supplant God's providential rule with his own. He is driven by jealousy, not envy. Hence, his grand urge to misworship is but the engendering of fine traditions, magnificent achievements, and beneficent inclinations yet all apart from the gracious endowments of God's order. Satan is a despot not unlike those that human experience attests: entranced by the false beauties, the false majesties, and the false virtues of independence from the Almighty.[7]

From the time of the temptation in the Garden to the present, the great satanic conspiracy has always been first and foremost to offer some sane, attractive, and wholesome counterfeit to the kingdom of God.

We must be clear on this matter: the consummation of evil is not best attained by getting us to drink blood from roiling cauldrons in debauched occult rites. Rather, it is as we are distracted from our providentially ordained callings—distracted by some interesting and enticing alternative.

Satan hopes to realize his ambition not merely by plunging individuals into bottomless pools of concupiscence but by gaining sway over the deepest affections and highest aspirations of this poor fallen world. He thus masquerades as an "angel of light," and his demonic minions appear as "servants of righteousness" (2 Cor. 11:13–15).

As Oswald Chambers has asserted: "This is his most cunning travesty . . . to counterfeit the Holy Spirit . . . to make men upright and individual—but seemingly self-governed and with no apparent need of God."[8]

In the process of implementing this credible and proficient alternative world system, much death and destruction certainly result. Defilement and debauchery are often inevitable when this wretched game is afoot. But these evils are not Satan's object. They are simply the second- and third-order consequences of his cultural coup. They are the lamentable hazards of any attempt to circumvent the consequences of the Fall.

The inclination of the ideological social engineers, like that of Satan, is to attempt a cosmic end run around the stark reality of the Fall. By all outward appearances, such a maneuver seems feasible. The rulers of most men's minds are not facts or statistics but general impressions, and like other rulers, general impressions are deposed only with the greatest difficulty.

But in the end, they are deposed. Of that we can be certain. False worldviews ultimately must collapse under the weight of their own absurdity. And so, history is filled with the broken relics of thousand-year Reichs, efficient Soviet collectives, social welfare democracies, Aryan paradises, and global *Ji'hads* that simply never *did* happen because they never *could* happen.

Kermit Roosevelt, the youngest son of Theodore Roosevelt, spent his life examining the problems of the Middle East. In 1949, he wrote prophetically:

> Are we yet aware of the danger that in the Middle East the United Nations may come to be regarded and mistrusted and hated as the guardian of the New World Order—the New Age trappings for the old Humanistic conspiracy of Left and Right together? The danger of Russia and the United States is the *seen* danger, and a grave one it is. Seen, it must in time be settled by peace or war. The danger of Orient versus Occident—of Islamic culture versus Christian culture—seems as yet *unseen*. That could be ruinous. We may well succumb to it from not seeing. We must not assume in the days ahead that the crisis in the Middle East can be solved through military alliances, political connivance, or strategic initiative. Beware of the politicians or the coalitions that propose such a solution—they may be fairly regarded, whether from the Left or the Right as a part of the same old entrenched interests that have stood against the Christian faith and have fought for a mechanical imposition of a new age or a new world order since the time of the Fall.[9]

An attempt to resurrect some kind of utopian new world order is not a solution to the crisis in the Middle East. Instead, it is part and parcel of the crisis. It is at the root of the crisis—with its only antidote being the faithful propagation of truth.

Chapter Nine

A Tale of Two Households

The world is at this moment passing through one of those terrible periods of convulsion when the souls of men and of nations are tried as by fire. Woe to the man or to the nation that at such a time stands as once Laodicea stood; as the people of ancient Meroz stood, when they dared not come to the help of the Lord against the mighty. In such a crisis the moral weakling is the enemy of the right, the enemy of life, liberty, and the pursuit of happiness.

—THEODORE ROOSEVELT[1]

American foreign policy around the world and in the Middle East during the last century has been, for all intents and purposes, the tale of two households. During the first half of the century, it was guided by the principles and precepts of the Roosevelts of Sagamore Hill. During the second half, it was guided by the principles and precepts of the Roosevelts of Hyde Park. The difference between the two was profound and has left a lasting impress upon the world in which we live.[2]

Theodore Roosevelt, the patriarch of the Sagamore Hill side of the family, was a remarkable man of unbounded energies and many careers. Before his fiftieth birthday he had served the Republican Party as a New York state legislator; he had been the undersecretary of the navy, the police commissioner for the city of New York, the United States Civil Service commissioner, the governor of New York, the vice president serving with President William McKinley, and a colonel in the United States Army; and he held two terms as president of the United States. In addition, he had written nearly thirty books, run a cattle ranch in the Dakota territories, and conducted scientific expeditions on four continents. He was a brilliant man who read at least five books every week of his life. He was a physical man who enjoyed hunting, boxing, and wrestling. He was a spiritual man who took his faith very seriously and for years taught Sunday school in his Dutch Reformed church. And he was a family man who lovingly raised five children and enjoyed a lifelong romance with his wife.

His distant cousin, Franklin D. Roosevelt, was the patriarch of the Hyde Park side of the family. He, too, was a remarkable man. A Harvard-educated lawyer, he began his political career as a Democratic Party reformer in the New York state senate. His vigorous campaign on behalf of Woodrow Wilson—against his famous cousin—during the 1912 presidential election earned him an appointment as the assistant secretary of the navy. In 1920 he was the vice presidential running mate on the losing Democratic ticket. Eight years later, after a disabling bout with polio, he was elected to the first of two terms as New York's governor. In 1932 he ran for the presidency against the Depression-plagued Herbert Hoover and won overwhelmingly. During his record four terms, he directed the ambitious transformation of American government, guided the nation through World War II, and laid the foundations for the United Nations.

Neither TR nor FDR was an isolationist in his foreign policy formulations, at least not in the same sense that Charles Lindbergh or Robert Taft was. Both believed that America should play a significant role in the international community of nations. Both believed that America was the fulcrum of the modern world—that American strength, ingenuity, and principles should be exported to the farthest ends of the earth.

Even so, their differences were very significant. TR was a nationalist. FDR was an internationalist.

TR was a reformer who wanted to firmly and faithfully reestablish the old world order. FDR was a revolutionary who wanted to boldly and unashamedly usher in a new world order.

TR's motto was "walk softly and carry a big stick." FDR's motto was "good neighbors live in solidarity."

TR spoke forcefully but led the world into a remarkable epoch of peace; he even won the Nobel Peace Prize in 1906. Like his mentor Woodrow Wilson, FDR spoke of peace but led the world into the bloodiest confrontation in man's tortured history.

The difference between these two perspectives was fundamental and presuppositional. Whereas FDR's expansive global vision was informed by an unhesitatingly humanistic worldview, TR's focused civic vision was informed by an uncompromising Christian worldview. In fact, while FDR rejected the faith of his fathers early in life, TR stood foursquare on the legacy of biblical orthodoxy. He often asserted that he was "proud of my Holland, Huguenot, and Covenanting ancestors, and proud that the blood of that stark Puritan divine Jonathan Edwards flows in the veins" of his children.

The practical outworking of these two models for American foreign policy was dramatic: FDR's led to bureaucracy, insecurity, and inefficiency at home, and war, tyranny, and neo-imperialism abroad. TR's led to prosperity, sagacity, and safety at home, and peace, liberty, and cooperation abroad.

Of the two perspectives, TR's was by far the more desirable and by far the more biblical—adhering as it did to the mandate passed down by the Old Testament prophet Micah.

The Micah Mandate

In 1917, when American troops were preparing to sail across the sea to take to the battlefields of France and Belgium in the First World War, the New York Bible Society asked TR to inscribe a message in the pocket New Testaments that each soldier would be given. The great man happily complied:

The teaching of the New Testament is foreshadowed in Micah's verse: "What more doth the Lord require of thee than to *do justice*, and to *love mercy*, and to *walk humbly* with thy God." *Do justice*; and therefore fight valiantly against those that stand for the reign of Moloch and Beelzebub on this earth. *Love mercy*; treat your enemies well; succor the afflicted; treat every woman as if she were your sister; care for the little children; and be tender with the old and helpless. *Walk humbly*; you will do so if you study the life and teachings of the Savior, walking in His steps. And remember: the most perfect machinery of government will not keep us as a nation from destruction if there is not within us a soul. No abounding of material prosperity shall avail us if our spiritual senses atrophy. The foes of our own household will surely prevail against us unless there be in our people an inner life which finds its outward expression in a morality like unto that preached by the seers and prophets of God when the grandeur that was Greece and the glory that was Rome still lay in the future.[3]

TR understood only too well the essence of biblical ethics as it applied to public policy. He understood that the security of men and nations depends on faithful adherence to Micah's threefold demonstration of discipleship: a strident commitment to the just application of law (Rom. 2:11–24; James 2:8–13), a practical concern for the unfortunate (James 1:27; Phil. 2:4), and a reverent fear of almighty God (Prov. 1:7; Acts 10:34–35). He knew that even with the deployment of superior forces in superior numbers with superior armaments, the American armies would ultimately be defeated during the war if they took to the field bereft of these essential spiritual resources. TR self-consciously integrated these three standards into his foreign policy framework, thus creating a paradigm well worth emulating.

The Standard of Justice

During his tenure in Washington with the Civil Service Commission, TR wrote a biography of Gouverneur Morris—the notable merchant, lawyer, and planter from Pennsylvania who drafted the final version of the Constitution. TR, like Morris, believed that in order for the American experiment in liberty to succeed, justice and righteousness had to be welded together as one in the hearts and minds of the citizenry. He was fond of quoting Morris's famous maxim on the subject: "Liberty and justice simply cannot be had apart from the gracious influences of a righteous people. A righteous people simply cannot exist apart from the aspiration to liberty and justice. The Christian religion and its incumbent morality is tied to the cause of freedom with a Gordian knot; loose one from the other and both are sent asunder."[4]

Throughout the Bible, the attributes of justice and righteousness are inextricably linked. In more than sixty passages across the wide span of the Old and New Testaments, God's Word makes it plain that to attempt to secure life, liberty, and the pursuit of happiness apart from the clearly revealed ethical parameters of goodness, truth, purity, faithfulness, and holiness is utter folly. On the other hand, a people who diligently seek to do righteousness will inevitably pursue justice as well. The two go together. One cannot be had without the other.

Again and again the refrain sounds:

> This is what the LORD says:
> "Maintain justice and do what is right,
> for my salvation is close at hand
>   and my righteousness will soon be revealed."
>   (Isa. 56:1 NIV)

> The LORD loves righteousness and justice. (Ps. 33:5 NIV)

> Righteousness and justice are the foundation of [the Lord's]
>   throne; love and faithfulness go before [Him.]
>   (Ps. 89:14 NIV)

> In faithfulness he will bring forth justice. (Isa. 42:3 NIV)

> [He says:] I will make justice the measuring line and righ-
>   teousness the plumb line. (Isa. 28:17 NIV)

> Blessed are they who maintain justice,
>   who constantly do what is right. (Ps. 106:3 NIV)

> Learn to do right!
> Seek justice. (Isa. 1:17 NIV)

Hate evil, love good;
   maintain justice . . .
Perhaps the LORD God Almighty will have mercy.
   (Amos 5:15 NIV)

Let justice roll on like a river,
   righteousness like a never-failing stream! (Amos 5:24 NIV)

Because Jesus emphasized this very unity between moral purity and judicial integrity in His earthly ministry, He continually found Himself in conflict with the religious leaders and the secularists of His day. Neither cared for His biblically rooted insistence that justice was impossible apart from righteousness, and vice versa.

TR recognized and reasserted this connection between justice and righteousness. He stood steadfast against the secular tendency to remove morality from the arena of justice; he was equally vigilant in opposing the religious tendency to remove justice from the arena of spirituality.

The Standard of Mercy

During his campaign speeches in 1912, TR often liked to quote the great American journalist, pastor, and statesman during the founding era, Morgan Fraser, who said,

No tyrant can ere long rule a gracious and merciful people. Charity sows seeds of freedom that may not be suppressed, for charity naturally disposes authority to the charitable, and the charitable are naturally disposed to freedom. Thus, when the people of the Living God undertake the holy duty of caring for the needy, the poor, the brokenhearted, and the deprived, the perverse subverters of morality, truth and liberty are certain to be exposed and deposed.[5]

To TR, this summarized his own ambition for America: to become rich in authority by becoming rich in service—to become great by becoming good.

One of the most basic principles of the Christian worldview is that the ability to lead a society is earned, not inherited. And it is earned through faithful, compassionate, and merciful service. Whoever becomes the benefactor of the people will ultimately be able to wield authority with them (Luke 22:25).

Jesus said, "Blessed are the merciful, for they shall receive mercy" (Matt. 5:7). That is why He lived His life as a servant (Luke 22:27). He came to serve, not to be served (Matt. 20:28). He came offering mercy at every turn (Matt. 9:13; Mark 5:19).

Not surprisingly He called His disciples to a similar life of selfless giving (Luke 22:26). He called us to be servants (Matt. 19:30). He said, "Whoever wishes to be chief among you, let him be your servant" (Matt. 20:27). He said, "Be merciful, just as your Father is merciful" (Luke 6:36). The attitude of all aspiring leaders should be the same as that of Christ Jesus:

Who, being in very nature God,
    did not consider equality with God something to be
    grasped,
but made himself nothing,
    taking the very nature of a servant. (Phil. 2:5–7 NIV)

TR believed, based on this biblical principle, that our nation's activities abroad ought not to be motivated by greed, avarice, pragmatism, tradition, or any other artificial standard. Instead, they ought to be motivated by what is right and good and true. That is the confident posture of the servant leader—neither promiscuously acquiescent nor pompously irascible.

The Standard of Humility

In the days before American involvement in World War I, when the crisis of the Middle East had once again taken the world's center stage, TR urged the nation and its leaders to recognize the full dimensions of the conflict:

> Prayer is our greatest weapon in these or any other times. Best we not send our boys across the sea to face the heathen hordes lest we have a nation at home one in prayer. If history teaches us nothing else, let us at least remember what the Byzantines learned, what the Crusaders learned, and what the French learned: you cannot face the dread terror of Islam in mere human strength. When the quietude of the desert has been stirred, let all Christian men and women turn to the sovereign Lord. Let all Christian men and women turn to Him in holy seasons of prayer.[6]

In calling on the American people to recognize the spiritual dimensions of the conflict in the Middle East, TR was merely reiterating the philosophy of his hero, George Washington, who asserted, "It is the first duty of all nations to acknowledge the providence of almighty God, to obey His will, to be grateful for

His benefits, and to humbly implore His protection and favor in holy fear."[7]

Washington added,

Of all the dispositions and habits which lead to civil prosperity, a humble fear before the Almighty and a life of Christian morality are indispensable supports. In vain would that man claim the attribute of patriotism, who should labor to subvert these great pillars of human happiness, these firmest props of the duties of men and citizens. A volume could not trace all their connections with private and public felicity. Let it simply be stated that there is no security for property, for reputation, or for life, if the sense of religious obligation desert the oaths, which are the instruments of investigation in courts of true justice.[8]

TR and Washington understood that the most realistic approach to an issue—to any issue—is always theocentric. In other words, it begins and ends with a recognition that the Lord is the Alpha and the Omega of the whole created order (Rev. 1:8) and that He exercises His sovereign control over it at all times and in all places (Ps. 115:3).

The Bible is prolific in its assertion of this truth:

The fear of the LORD is the beginning of wisdom;
A good understanding have all those who do His
    commandments;
His praise endures forever. (Ps. 111:10)

The fear of the LORD is the beginning of knowledge,
Fools despise wisdom and instruction. (Prov. 1:7)

The fear of the LORD prolongs life,
But the years of the wicked will be shortened. (Prov. 10:27)

In the fear of the LORD there is strong confidence,
And His children will have a place of refuge.
The fear of the LORD is a fountain of life,
To turn one away from the snares of death.
   (Prov. 14:26–27 NKJV)

Better is a little with the fear of the LORD,
Than great treasure with trouble. (Prov. 15:16 NKJV)

Clothe yourselves with humility toward one another, for God is opposed to the proud, but gives grace to the humble. Humble yourselves, therefore, under the mighty hand of God, that He may exalt you at the proper time, casting all your anxiety on Him, because He cares for you. (1 Peter 5:5–7)

A nation whose leaders are humbled in fear before God will suffer no want (Ps. 34:9). It will surely be blessed (Ps. 115:13). And it will be set high above all the nations of the earth (Deut. 28:1).

This is the fundamental truth that underlies the Christian worldview and the motivation that drove TR's approach to foreign policy in the Middle East.

Prophecy and the Cultural Mandate

There are doomsayers, and there are naysayers. The doomsayers argue that the end is upon us, the last days have come, the sky is falling, and all is lost. The naysayers argue that there is nothing to worry about, everything is under control, things can only get better, and the New Age is nigh unto us.

Neither perspective is biblical. And neither perspective is responsible.

After the ascension of Christ, the disciples were awestruck—staring into the clouds. In short order, though, two angelic messengers came and rebuked them: "Men of Galilee, why do you stand gazing up into heaven?" (Acts 1:11 NKJV).

Jesus had given them a job to do. But there they were paralyzed with wonder. Jesus had called them to evangelize the world. But there they were loitering in recalcitrance. Jesus had promised them power and unction. But there they were frozen in the grips of hysteria. Jesus had commanded them to occupy the earth until He returned. But there they were occupied only with their own wild speculations.

Little has changed for too many of Christ's disciples. They are still looking "steadfastly toward heaven" (Acts 1:10 NKJV) instead of fulfilling their mandate to win the world with justice, mercy, and humility.

Theodore Roosevelt had little patience for either doomsayers or naysayers. He built a foreign policy on the notion that Christ meant what He had said. Can we do anything less?

In January 1776, George Wythe of Virginia asked John Adams to draw up a plan that would enable the American colonies to establish a constitutional system strong enough to survive the rigors of war with England and to meet the challenges of the months and years that followed. Adams replied with his usual discernment, discretion, and wisdom:

The foundation of every nation is some principle or passion in the minds of the people. The noblest principles and most generous affections in our Christian character, then, have the fairest chance to support the noblest and the most generous models of civil covenant. If liberty and justice for all men is to be ensured then we cannot, we dare not, we must not stray from the Writ of right.[9]

Ideas have consequences. Worldviews make a difference. Covenants alter the course of cultures and ultimately all of history. To fail to realize this basic and fundamental truth is to miss the import of social relations in this poor fallen world altogether.

Does it take a Teddy Roosevelt to do justice, love mercy, and walk humbly with our God? Of course not. It is a pattern for life and liberty that we all can and should follow. Sometimes it just takes a T R to show us that such things are actually possible, that they are worth fighting for, and that they are worth living out.

Chapter Ten

The End of the Beginning

We belong to quite as many regiments as the German Kaiser. Our regiments are regiments that are embattled everywhere; they fight an unending fight against all that is hopeless and rapacious and of evil report. The only difference is that we have the regiments, but not the uniforms.

—G. K. CHESTERTON[1]

The sun rose over the Kidron Valley in deep shades of scarlet. From my hotel window I could see the Old City begin to come to life, its austere enchantment scarred and fluted with the trampled paths of the eons.

Below me I saw a small cluster of tourists—an all-too-uncommon sight in these dire days of *Intifada* strikes, terrorist attacks, and suicide bombings. They walked toward the Jaffa Gate very slowly, as if savoring every precious morsel of time and space. An air of sanctity clothed them. They seemed hushed by awe. It is deep in man to love the place where Divinity has walked. To pray there. To tread these streets and to touch these stones. It offers us a momentary communion. And so the holy sites multiply under our fervor, however tenuous their roots in history.

A few blocks from where the tourists walked, a quiet procession made its way toward the entrance to the Church of the Holy Sepulcher. Monks with long gnarled beards and cloaked in fraying robes held their tapers before them, cherishing their heritage as a fountain in the emptiness. The sweet fragrance of their censers and the haunting refrains of their chants echoed through the narrow streets anointing the secular with the sacred.

Still deeper into the city, beyond the ancient battlements of Suleiman, the *Hasidim* were gathering for prayer at the Western Wall. They were clearly people in the ebb tide of tradition. A few of the men wore startling robes of fawn, belted at the waist like dressing gowns, but most of them were veiled entirely in dusty black—thin, long coats and wide, perched hats. Their unbarbered beards gushed in all directions. Their sun-gingered ringlets either curled around their ears or dangled like guilt-cords in the sanctuary. Their faces were gaunt with the tautness of the ghetto. With their prayer shawls unfurled, they cried out to Jehovah in unison and in separate voices—the irony of which is the essence of the Judaic community and its worship.

And above them, on the wraith of Herod's temple—the paved loneliness of a mountain plateau—a ragged line of the *Umma* walked silently into the shrine of Muhammad's mysterious transport. Under its vast, empty dome, the pious souls went through their actions carefully. They stood, they touched their foreheads to the ground in prayer, they clasped their hands on their stomachs, and they patted their knees. There was nothing self-conscious in their gestures. Their humility was genuine—expressed in a formal and dignified service unchanged by the passing of centuries.

I saw all this from the vantage of my window and was struck with wonder. I wondered how such a place could engender such bitter rivalry, such cruel animus, and such callous horror. How could this place of devotion be the spawning ground of global terrorism?

It was then that I recalled my catechism lessons on the effects of the Fall, on the breadth and depth of depravity, and on the pervasive reach of sin. It was then that deep within I heard the mournful echo of the ancient cantor's plea:

> Jerusalem is built
> As a city that is compact together,
> Where the tribes go up,
> The tribes of the LORD,
> To the Testimony of Israel,
> To give thanks to the name of the LORD.
> For thrones are set there for judgment,
> The thrones of the house of David.
> Pray for the peace of Jerusalem. (Ps. 122:3–6 NKJV)

As I turned from the casement, I realized that the peace of Jerusalem would never—and could never—be realized out of the cacophony of either human ambition or devotion. It would not—and could not—be achieved by the desperate souls below me. Waging peace is always a more treacherous affair than waging war. It can be realized only by fealty to Christ:

> Why do the nations rage,
> And the people plot a vain thing?
> The kings of the earth set themselves,
> And the rulers take counsel together,
> Against the LORD and against His Anointed, saying,
> "Let us break Their bonds in pieces

And cast away Their cords from us."
He who sits in the heavens shall laugh;
The LORD shall hold them in derision.
Then He shall speak to them in His wrath,
And distress them in His deep displeasure:
"Yet I have set My King
On My holy hill of Zion."
"I will declare the decree:
The LORD has said to Me,
'You are My Son,
Today I have begotten You.
Ask of Me, and I will give You
The nations for Your inheritance,
And the ends of the earth for Your possession.
You shall break them with a rod of iron;
You shall dash them to pieces like a potter's vessel.'"
Now therefore, be wise, O kings;
Be instructed, you judges of the earth.
Serve the LORD with fear,
And rejoice with trembling.
Kiss the Son, lest He be angry,
And you perish in the way,
When His wrath is kindled but a little.
Blessed are all those who put their trust in Him.

   (Ps. 2:1–12 NKJV)

Notes

Introduction

1. G. K. Chesterton, *A Chesterton Anthology* (London: Sheed and Ward, 1937), 121.

2. Charles Haddon Spurgeon, *John Ploughman's Pictures* (Philadelphia: John Altemus, 1901), 137.

3. Hilaire Belloc, *Stories, Essays, and Poems* (London: J. M. Dent, 1952), 72.

4. Spurgeon, *John Ploughman's Pictures,* 137.

5. "To God alone, be the glory. Jesus, save us."

Chapter One

1. Winston Churchill, *Maxims and Quips* (London: Standard Limited, 1978).

2. *New Yorker,* 24 September 2001.

3. *International Herald Tribune,* 14 September 2001.

4. James Callahan, *The Fords* (Detroit: Motor City Press, 1967), 128.

5. *Ibid.*

6. *Ibid.*

7. *Newsweek*, 6 July 1970.

8. *Ibid.*

9. Tim Dowley, ed., *Eerdmans' Handbook to the History of Christianity* (Grand Rapids, MI: Eerdmans, 1977), 2.

10. *Ibid.*

11. Michael Laughton-Douglas, *Truer Truth Than This* (London: Haverford, 1978), 84.

12. *Church History*, February 1990.

13. *Ibid.*

14. Stephen Mansfield, *More Than Dates and Dead People* (Nashville: Cumberland House, 2000).

Chapter Two

1. George and Karen Grant, *Lost Causes* (Franklin, TN: Cumberland House, 1999), 48.

2. *New Yorker*, 24 September 2001.

3. *Ibid.*

4. *Ibid.*

5. *New York Post*, 14 September 2001.

6. *Sportsliner*, 2 October 2001.

7. *Ibid.*

8. *Ibid.*

Part 2, Opening Page

1. Frederick Thompson, *A World of Verse* (New York: Paige and Sons, 1939), 219.

Chapter Three

1. Rudyard Kipling, *Complete Verse* (New York: Doubleday, Doran, and Company, 1944), 233.

2. *International Herald Tribune,* 14 September 2001.

3. *New Yorker,* 24 September 2001.

4. *Ibid.*

5. *International Herald Tribune,* 27 September 2001.

6. *WorldNetDaily,* 2 October 2001.

7. *Ibid.*

8. *Ibid.*

9. Hilaire Belloc, *The Great Heresies* (London: Sheed and Ward, 1938), 47.

10. *Time,* 1 October 2001.

11. *Time,* 11 January 1999.

12. E. F. Schumacher, *Small Is Beautiful* (New York: Harper and Row, 1975), 52.

13. Alvin Toffler, *Future Shock* (New York: Bantam, 1971), 158.

14. Schumacher, *Small Is Beautiful,* 52.

15. James Sire, *How to Read Slowly* (Wheaton, IL: Harold Shaw, 1978), 14–15.

16. Genesis 4:3–8; Hebrews 11:4; 1 John 3:12.

17. Numbers 31:16; 2 Peter 2:15; Revelation 2:14.

18. Numbers 16:1–3, 31–35.

Chapter Four

1. Al Hurriya, *From Nebuchadnezzar to Saddam Hussein: Babylon Rises Again,* 4th ed. (Baghdad: Iraqi Ministry of Information and Culture, 1987, 1990), 7.

2. *Ibid.,* 9.

3. *Ha Ubal Or* (Jerusalem edition), 3 January 1991.

4. *Ibid.*

5. James L. Baehr, *Leadership in the East: An Examination of the Passing Patriarchal Order* (Boston: Society of Political Science University Studies, 1973), 127–28.

6. *Al Watan Kuwait,* 4 October 1981.

7. *Ibid.*

8. *Al Sha'ab Cairo,* 17 August 2001.

9. Thomas W. Lippman, *Understanding Islam* (New York: New American Library, 1982), 116.

10. *Ibid.,* 117.

11. *Ibid.*

12. *Ibid.*

Chapter Five

1. Andrew Nelson Lytle, *Sketches* (Nashville, TN: Pivot Press, 1967), 4.

2. *The Middle East Business Report,* November 1990.

3. *Ha Ubal Or* (Jerusalem edition), 3 January 1991.

4. *Ibid.*

5. Louis R. Essher, *Exile and Exodus: The Jewish-British Regiments in World War II* (London: Jackson-Poore, 1961), 84.

6. *New Dimensions Magazine,* January 1991.

7. *Ibid.*

8. *Ibid.*

9. *Ha Ubal Or* (Jerusalem edition), 3 January 1991.

10. *Ibid.*

11. *Jerusalem Post,* 14 December 1990.

12. *Ibid.*

13. *The PLO: Has It Complied with Its Commitments?* (Israel: Ministry of Foreign Affairs, August 1990), 20.

14. *Al Qabas Kuwait,* 19 December 1989.

Chapter Six

1. Grant, *Lost Causes,* 97.

2. *The Glory of Byzantine Rome* (Zagreb, Croatia: Orthodox International Press, 1979), 37.

3. *Ibid.*, 39.

4. *Ibid.*, 62.

5. *Al Sha'ab Cairo*, July 1982.

6. George Grant, *The Last Crusader* (Wheaton, IL: Crossway Books, 1992), 59.

7. *Ibid.*, 60.

8. *The Dhimmi Newsletter*, October 1990.

9. Iman Khomeini, *Excerpts from Speeches and Messages of Iman Khomeini on the Unity of Muslims* (Tehran: Ministry of Islamic Guidance, 1979), 2.

10. *Ibid.*, 4.

11. *Ibid.*, 5.

12. *Ibid.*, 4.

13. Lester Mayfield-Owen, *Foxholes, Faith, and the First World War* (Phoenix, AZ: Liberty Bell Publishing House, 1971), 97.

Chapter Seven

1. Theodore Roosevelt, *Maxims, Speeches, and Correspondence* (New York: Patterson and Lusk, 1917), 88.

2. Martin Forbes, *History Lessons: The Importance of Cultural Memory* (New York: Palamir Publications, 1981), 112.

3. *Ibid.*, 113.

4. G. K. Chesterton, *Orthodoxy* (Garden City, NY: Image Books, 1959), 81.

Part 3, Opening Page

1. Houston MacGaverty, *Reformation Truth* (Tulsa: Reform Press, 1961), 2.

Chapter Eight

1. Xavier Ullert, *Episodic American Greatness* (Princeton, NJ: Claxton Press, 1977), 349.

2. Paul Johnson, *Intellectuals* (New York: Harper and Row, 1989), 1–2.

3. *Ibid.*

4. William Gairdner, *The War Against the Family* (Toronto: Stoddart, 1992), 6.

5. Michael H. Larour, *The Inklings and Their Influences* (London: S.F.G. & L. Presentations, 1986), 9.

6. Paul Johnson, *Modern Times: The World from the Twenties to the Eighties* (New York: Harper & Row, 1983), 689.

7. Richard B. Wagner, *Early Lutheran Missions* (Fredricksburg, TX: Wittenburg, 1971), 51–52.

8. Michael Lourdes, *The Holiness Movement in England* (London: Christian Light, 1980), 25.

9. David L. Johnson, *Theodore Roosevelt: American Monarch* (Philadelphia: American History Sources, 1981), 191.

Chapter Nine

1. Roosevelt, *Maxims, Speeches, and Correspondence*, 88.

2. For a further development of the theme of this chapter, see George Grant, *Carry a Big Stick* (Nashville, TN: Cumberland House, 1996).

3. Theodore Roosevelt, *Foes of Our Own Household* (New York: Charles Scribner's Sons, 1917), 3.

4. James Carter Braxton, *Gouverneur Morris: A Biographical Sketch* (Charleston, SC: Braden-Lowell Press, 1911), 99.

5. Morgan Fraser, *Sermons, Discourses, and Essays* (New York: Braun and Cie, 1921), 63.

6. Johnson, *Theodore Roosevelt: American Monarch*, 193.

7. Evan Davis, *Our Greatest President* (New York: Bedford Company, Publishers, 1891), 361.

8. *Ibid.*, 366.

9. Lamar P. Poirot, *The Adams Family: Four Generations of Service* (Quincy, MA: Truther and Forbes, Publishers, 1921), 109.

Chapter Ten

1. Chesterton, *Orthodoxy*, 82.

Acknowledgments

1. Samuel Johnson, *An Omnibus of His Wit and Wisdom* (London: Carrel Brothers, 1966), 43.

2. Justin Albertson, *The Scholastic Method* (Bloomington, IN: Caveat Publications, 1988), 3.

3. Roosevelt, *Foes of Our Own Household,* 137.

Glossary

The difference between the right word and the almost right word
is like the difference between lightning and the lightning bug.

—MARK TWAIN

Al Aqsa: The mosque in East Jerusalem that stands on or near
the site of Herod's temple just above the Wailing Wall.

Al Qaeda: The revolutionary terrorist network established by
Osama bin Laden; literally, "the base" or "beginning."

Allah: The name of the chief pagan Arabian god; adopted by
Muhammad for his monotheistic faith.

Arianism: A fourth-century Christian heresy; denied the Trinity.

Assassini: The special terror corps of the Islamic military resistance to Crusaders from the West; trained assassins.

Ayatollah: An honorific title in Shi'ite Islam for a revered
Mullah or Imam.

Aza'sin: The process of "cleansing" a region of infidelity; a form
of *Ji'had.*

Blood of the Moon: A foreboding prophetic term used in both
the Koran and the Bible; an image portending judgment.

Caliph: The successors to Muhammad; leaders of Islam.

Caliphate: The establishment of a caliph's rule.

Crusades: Attempts of Christian soldiers to recapture territory from Muslim conquerors; a movement lasting from the eleventh to the sixteenth centuries.

Dhimma: Submission tax imposed on subject nations; property confiscation; an alternative to *Ji'had.*

Fad'lak: A special travel tax imposed upon subject peoples; part of *Dhimma.*

Fatwah: A decree of anathema; a call for *Ji'had;* justification for the use of *Fidah'is.*

Fidah'is: Suicide assassins offered the rewards of martyrdom during *Ji'had.*

Hadith: An anthology of the sayings, stories, and legends of Muhammad; the second most important book in Islam behind the Koran.

Haj: The once-in-a-lifetime pilgrimage to Mecca every Muslim must make; one of the Five Pillars of Islam.

Hejaz: A region of the Arabian Peninsula.

Hijra: The exile of Muhammad to Medina.

Imam: A teacher of the Islamic faith and leader of a local or regional mosque.

Intifada: An insurrection or rebellion against unjust authority; justification for *Ji'had.*

Janissaries: Conscripted soldiers; served the Ottoman rulers as an elite fighting force, palace guards, and assassins.

Ji'had: One of the essential duties of Islam outlined in the Koran; literally: holy war.

Ji'zya: A special poll tax imposed upon subject peoples; part of *Dhimma.*

Ka'ba: An ancient pagan pantheon in Mecca dedicated to all gods; later appropriated by Muhammad as the center of Islamic worship; now the heart of the Holy Mosque.

Kafir: Any unbeliever or infidel: Christian, Jew, or pagan.

Khar'aj: A special property tax imposed upon subject peoples; part of *Dhimma.*

Koran: An anthology of the 114 prophecies of Muhammad; the scriptures of the Islamic faith.

Mahdi: A near-messianic figure in Islam; literally: a divinely inspired prophet.

Mecca: An Arabian commercial and trading center where Muhammad was born, raised, and received his prophecies; the holy city of Islam and site of the *Haj* pilgrimage.

Medina: An Arabian city in the Yathrib region of the Hejaz where Muhammad spent his years of exile.

Monophysitism: Fourth-century Christian heresy; denied the doctrine of the Trinity by over-emphasizing the deity of Christ.

Mosque: Place of prayer; used for teaching each Friday during corporate *Salat.*

Mount Hira: The mountain outside Mecca where Muhammad received his prophecies.

Mufti: The chief Imam of a city or region.

Mujaheddin: Afghan freedom fighters against Russian occupation.

Mullah: A leader of one or another of the various movements within Islam; a highly regarded teacher of Islam recognized by his peers.

Nestorianism: Fourth-century Christian heresy; denied the doctrine of the Trinity by over-emphasizing the humanity of Christ.

Pillars: The five essential disciplines of Islamic practice: *Shahada, Salat, Zakat, Haj,* and *Saum.*

Rakatin Prayer: A series of nods, bows, and prostrations toward Mecca during *Salat.*

Ramadan: A month of daytime fasting from all food and drink.

Razzia: A form of internal war against apostasy; rebellion against unjust rulers who violate Koranic law; justification for the use of *Fidah'is.*

Reconquesta: The recovery of the Iberian Peninsula from the Muslim conquerors by Christian Crusaders from the tenth through the fifteenth centuries; completed in 1492.

Riddah: A civil war fought for the sake of the purity of the faith and the defense of the Holy Mosques in Mecca and Medina; justification for the use of *Fidah'is.*

Salat: The five-times-daily Rakatin prayer and worship of the Muslim; one of the Five Pillars of Islam.

Saum: The daytime fasting ritual of a Muslim during the month of Ramadan; one of the Five Pillars of Islam.

Shabat: The Jewish Sabbath.

Shahada: The profession of faith—"There is no god but Allah and Muhammad is his prophet"—to be offered daily by every Muslim; one of the Five Pillars of Islam.

Shi'ite: A strict branch of fundamentalist Islamic practice; predominates in Iran.

Souq: A marketplace.

Sufi: A branch of Islam rooted in mysticism and ecstatic experience.

Sult'ah: A discretionary sultan's tax imposed upon subject peoples; part of *Dhimma.*

Sunni: The main branch of Islam; includes most moderates and some fundamentalists.

Suras: The 114 individual prophecies or liturgical units within the Koran.

Taliban: The fundamentalist ruling militia of Afghanistan; literally, "seekers of truth" or "students."

Umma: A true Muslim believer.

Wahhabi: The strict branch of Sunni Islam practiced in Saudi Arabia.

Zakat: The pious Muslim discipline of almsgiving and the disposition of property; one of the Five Pillars of Islam.

Zoroastrianism: Ancient Persian dualistic religion; a complex doctrine of physics and metaphysics, closely tied to astronomy and the Magi of the East.

Bibliography

Just as art needs no justification—we may rest assured that beauty, goodness, and truth are well able to fend for themselves—so also the shelf life needs no defense. Mere affirmation affords stark contrast enough with the howling wasteland of modern bohemianism.

—Tristan Gylberd

Armstrong, Karen. *Islam: A History.* New York, Modern Library, 2000.

———. *Muhammad: A Biography of the Prophet.* San Francisco: HarperCollins, 1993.

Bakhash, Shaul. *The Reign of the Ayatollahs: Iran and the Islamic Revolution.* New York: Basic Books, 1984, 1986.

Belloc, Hilaire. *The Great Heresies.* London: Sheed and Ward, 1938.

———. *The Jews.* London: Butler and Tanner, 1922.

Bill, James A., and Carl Leiden. *The Middle East: Politics and Power.* Boston: Allyn and Bacon, 1974.

Bolitho, William. *Twelve Against the Gods: The Story of Adventure.* New York: Readers Club, 1941.

Burton, Sir Richard. *The Jew, The Gypsy and El Islam.* Allen and Davies, 1898.

Chesterton, G. K. *The Barbarism of Berlin*. London: Cassell and Company, 1914.

Chilton, David. *Paradise Restored: A Biblical Eschatology of Victory*. Fort Worth, TX: Dominion Press, 1985.

Collins, Larry, and Dominique Lapierre. *O Jerusalem!* London: Grafton Books, 1982.

Cook, Michael. *Muhammad*. New York: Oxford University Press, 1983.

Darsh, Dr. S. M. *Muslims in Europe*. London: Ta-Ha Publishers, 1980.

Dawood, N. J., trans. *Koran*. London: Penguin, 1956.

de Camp, L. Sprague. *The Ancient Engineers*. New York: Ballantine, 1963.

de Villiers, Gerard, Bernard Touchais, and Annick de Villiers. *The Imperial Shah: An Informal Biography*. Boston: Little, Brown, 1976.

Deacon, Richard. *The Israeli Secret Service*. New York: Sphere Books, 1979.

Durant, Will. *Our Oriental Heritage*. Vol. 1, *The Story of Civilization*. New York: Simon and Schuster, 1954.

Dyer, Charles. *The Rise of Babylon*. Wheaton, IL: Tyndale, 1991.

Fischer, Michael. *Iran: From Religious Dispute to Revolution*. Cambridge, MA: Harvard University Press, 1980.

Follett, Ken. *On Wings of Eagles*. New York: Signet, 1983.

Friedman, Thomas. *From Beirut to Jerusalem*. New York: Anchor Books, 1989.

Fromkin, David. *A Peace to End All Peace: The Fall of the Ottoman Empire and the Creation of the Modern Middle East.* New York: Avon Books, 1989.

Goode, Stephen. *The Prophet and the Revolutionary: Arab Socialism and the Modern Middle East.* New York: Franklin Watts, 1975.

Hamada, Louis Bahjat. *Understanding the Arab World.* Nashville, TN: Thomas Nelson, 1990.

Hamilton, Rita. *The Poem of the Cid.* Translated by Janet Perry. New York: Penguin, 1985.

Herzl, Theodor. *The Jewish State.* New York: Dover, 1946.

Herzog, Chaim. *The Arab-Israeli Wars: War and Peace in the Middle East from the War of Independence Through Lebanon.* New York: Vintage Books, 1984.

Hinnells, John R., ed. *A Handbook of Living Religions.* New York: Pelican Books, 1985.

Hodson, Peregrine. *Under the Sickle Moon.* New York: Atlantic Monthly Press, 1986.

Holt, P. M., Anne K. S. Lambton, and Bernard Lewis, eds. *The Cambridge History of Islam.* New York: Cambridge University Press, 1970.

Ibraham, Ishak. *Black Gold and Holy War.* Nashville, TN: Thomas Nelson, 1983.

Johnson, Paul. *A History of the Jews.* New York: Harper and Row, 1987.

Jordan, James B. *The Bible and the Nations.* Niceville, FL: Biblical Horizons, 1988.

Kajouri, Seth, tr. *The Koran and the Hadith: An English Translation for Christians and Jews.* Bethlehem, Israel: St. Catherine's Publication Society, 1988.

Kapuscinski, Ryszard. *Shah of Shahs.* New York: Vintage Books, 1982.

Khalil, Samir al. *Republic of Fear: The Inside Story of Saddam's Iraq.* New York: Pantheon, 1989.

Kinross, Lord. *The Ottoman Centuries: The Rise and Fall of the Turkish Empire.* New York: Marrow Quill, 1977.

Kritzeck, James, ed. *Anthology of Islamic Literature: From the Rise of Islam to Modern Times.* New York: New American Library, 1964.

Lamb, David. *The Arabs: Journeys Beyond the Mirage.* New York: Vintage Books, 1987.

Lancaster, Pat, ed. *Traveller's Guide to the Middle East.* Edison, NJ: Hunter Publishing, 1988.

Lapidus, Ira M. *A History of Islamic Societies.* New York: Cambridge University Press, 1988.

Lippman, Thomas. *Understanding Islam: An Introduction to the Moslem World.* New York: Mentor, 1982.

Loffreda, Stanislao. *Recovering Capharnaum.* Milano, Italy: Poligrafico Artioli Modena, 1985.

Lunt, James. *Hussein of Jordan.* London: Fontana, 1990.

Mace, John. *Modern Persian.* New York: Hodder and Stoughton, 1962.

Macfie, A. L. *The Eastern Question 1774–1923.* New York: Longman, 1989.

McDowell, Bruce, and Anees Zaka. *Muslims and Christians at the Table*. Phillipsburg, NJ: P & R Publishing, 1999.

McDowell, Josh, and John Gilchrist. *The Islam Debate*. San Bernardino, CA: Here's Life, 1983.

McKinnin, Dan. *Bullseye Iraq*. New York: Berkley Books, 1988.

Miller, Judith, and Laurie Mylroie. *Saddam Hussein and the Crisis in the Gulf*. New York: Times Books, 1990.

Mortimer, Edward. *Faith and Power: The Politics of Islam*. New York: Vintage Books, 1982.

Naipaul, V. S. *Among the Believers: An Islamic Journey*. New York: Vintage Books, 1981.

Newell, Richard S., and Nancy Peabody Newell. *The Struggle for Afghanistan*. Ithaca, NY: Cornell University Press, 1981.

Payne, Robert. *The Dream and the Tomb: A History of the Crusades*. New York: Stein and Day, 1984.

Pierce, James Wilson. *Story of Turkey and Armenia*. Baltimore: R. H. Woodward, 1896.

Pryce-Jones, David. *The Closed Circle: An Interpretation of the Arabs*. London: Paladin, 1990.

Reed, Douglas. *The Controversy of Zion*. Durban, Natal, South Africa: Dolphin Press, 1978.

Riley-Smith, Jonathan. *The Crusades: A Short History*. New Haven: Yale University Press, 1987.

Rivers, Gayle. *The War Against the Terrorists: How to Win It*. New York: Stein and Day, 1986.

Rivers, Gayle, and James Hudson. *The Teheran Contract*. New York: Bantam Books, 1982.

Roosevelt, Kermit. *Countercoup: The Struggle for the Control of Iran*. New York: McGraw-Hill, 1979.

Rubin, Barry. *Paved with Good Intentions: The American Experience and Iran*. New York: Penguin, 1982.

Runciman, Steven. *The Fall of Constantinople 1453*. New York: Cambridge University Press, 1965.

———. *The First Crusade and the Foundations of the Kingdom of Jerusalem: A History of the Crusades*. New York: Cambridge University Press, 1951.

———. *The Kingdom of Jerusalem and the Frankish East 1100–1187: A History of the Crusades*. New York: Cambridge University Press, 1952.

———. *The Kingdom of Acre and the Later Crusades: A History of the Crusades*. New York: Cambridge University Press, 1954.

———. *The Great Church in Captivity: A Study of the Patriarchate of Constantinople from the Eve of the Turkish Conquest to the Greek War of Independence*. New York: Cambridge University Press, 1968.

Ryan, Paul B. *The Iranian Rescue Mission: Why It Failed*. Annapolis, MD: Naval Institute Press, 1985.

Saikal, Amin. *The Rise and Fall of the Shah*. Princeton, NJ: Princeton University Press, 1980.

Sanders, N. K. *The Epic of Gilgamesh*. New York: Penguin, 1960.

Sayers, Dorothy L., trans. *The Song of Roland*. New York: Penguin, 1957.

Sick, Gary. *All Fall Down: America's Tragic Encounter with Iran*. New York: Random House, 1985.

Simpson, John. *Behind Iranian Lines: Travels Through Revolutionary Iran and the Persian Past.* London: Fontana, 1989.

Sivan, Emmanuel. *Radical Islam: Medieval Theology and Modern Politics.* New Haven: Yale University Press, 1990.

Stark, Freya. *The Journey's Echo.* New York: Echo Press, 1988.

Taheri, Amir. *The Spirit of Allah: Khomeini and the Islamic Revolution.* Bethesda, MD: Alder and Alder, 1986.

Theroux, Peter. *Sandstorms: Days and Nights in Arabia.* New York: Norton, 1990.

Tritton, A. S. *Islam: Belief and Practices.* New York: Hutchinson's University Library, 1951.

Tuchman, Barbara. *Bible and Sword: England and Palestine from the Bronze Age to Balfour.* New York: Ballantine, 1984.

Twain, Mark. *The Innocents Abroad.* New York: Signet, 1980.

Wallach, John, and Janet Wallach. *Still Small Voices.* New York: Citadel Press, 1990.

Wheeler, Tony. *West Asia on a Shoestring.* Berkeley, CA: Lonely Planet, 1990.

Widlanski, Michael. *Can Israel Survive a Palestinian State?* Jerusalem: Institute for Advanced Strategic and Political Studies, 1990.

Wright, Robin. *The Last Great Revolution: Turmoil and Transformation in Iran.* New York: Vintage Books, 2001.

Zaehner, R. C. *Hindu and Muslim Mysticism.* New York: Schocken Books, 1969.

Zakaria, Rafiq. *The Struggle Within Islam: The Conflict Between Religion and Politics.* New York: Penguin, 1988.

Acknowledgments

The greatest part of a writer's time is spent in reading, in order to write: a man will turn over half a library to make one book. Still, his greatest insights come not from his learning, but from his friends.

—SAMUEL JOHNSON[1]

Henry David Thoreau once remarked, "The scholar rarely writes as well as the farmer talks."[2] As I have undertaken the task of writing this book, the truth of that observation has struck me afresh. The many ordinary and extraordinary people who have contributed to my thinking—Thoreau's farmers and their modern kith and kin—may very well have been able to articulate the roots of the renewed crisis between Islam and Western civilization better than I could have. In any case, it is clear enough to me that without their many kindnesses this book would not have been possible.

Two of America's most incisive experts in Middle Eastern affairs, General Richard Secord and General Daniel Graham, took time out from their very hectic schedules to brief me on the geopolitical situation in the region as well as the basis for United States military and diplomatic policy. Similarly Joel Belz and Martin LaBeuf, visionary publishers of *World Magazine* and the *Middle East Business Report*, respectively, shared with me their informed insights and perspectives.

A number of Christian Arabs from Syria, Lebanon, Iraq, Egypt, Jordan, and Algeria helped me focus my research and hone my arguments. The lives and testimonies of Philip Hamid, Georges Corm, Rabit Shehadeh, Johan Neguib, Rachid Shahhat, and Laila Abou Saif remain a marvel to me.

Several Syrian, Iranian, Iraqi, and Afghan exiles shared with me not only their opinions and experiences, but also their warm hospitality and abiding friendship. I am particularly grateful for the time and efforts that Nayef al Barras, Ibraham Abu Ayyad, Muhammad Kamel, Sakib Aziz, and Arslan Qu'bi have invested in this project.

In Israel, my friends Offer Eshed, Dafna Furst, Reba Cohen, and Michael Miamon made my time in their strife-riven nation both fruitful and enjoyable. Several members of the Knesset were very helpful in providing data and insights generally unavailable to American journalists and in sharing openly their hopes and their fears for the generations to come. My special thanks go to Uzi Landau, Tzachi Hanegbi, and Elyakim Haetzni. In addition, General Joshua Sagi, former assistant director of Israeli Military Intelligence, was very generous with his time and personal perspective of the regional conflict.

Rana Ardaji, Dr. Wahib Dajani, Khalil Touma, and Nehaya al Helo, all leaders in the Palestinian *Intifada*, graciously briefed me on the problems faced by Arabs in the Judean and Samarian sectors of the West Bank. In addition, the editorial staff of *Al Fajr*, a Palestinian newspaper produced in Jerusalem, provided me with transcriptions and translations of hard-to-find Arabic documents, stories, and interviews that I could not possibly have obtained on my own.

While I was writing the first edition, James B. Jordan and

Michael Hyatt helped me sort through all the tangled theological issues that could very easily have stymied the project. Jim's insight on the connection between the Tower of Babel and the new world order, and Mike's insight into the plight of Arab Christians proved to be invaluable. I am grateful for their wisdom and their friendship.

Several of my colleagues and students served selflessly in thankless tasks during the researching, writing, and revising of this new edition. Jim Small accompanied me to the Middle East, taking care of security, itinerary, and a hundred other incidentals. Mark Horne worked long hours tracking down obscure details and collecting necessary bibliographic resources. Christy Shurden, Amy Shore, and Sharon Cahoon helped to digitally transcribe the old edition. And the entire Bannockburn community pitched in with its usual selflessness and graciousness.

As always, my family members have been tremendously supportive. They have withstood my many absences with grace, and they have shared fully in my calling and my vision. Any success this project may ever inure must surely be theirs.

Theodore Roosevelt, a man who was amazingly prolific and phenomenally successful throughout his life, once said, "No other success in life—not being President, or being wealthy, or going to college, or writing a book, or anything else—comes up to the success of the men and women who can feel that they have done their duty and that their children and grandchildren rise up to call them blessed."[3]

Recognizing that, I pray that what I *do* before the watching eyes of my family never supersedes what I *am*.

Autumn 2001
King's Meadow Library

About the Author

George Grant, Ph.D., D.Litt., is professor of Moral Philosophy at the King's Meadow Study Center, editor of the Stirling Bridge newsletter, coordinator of the Covenant Classical School Association, and instructor at Franklin Classical School, Knox Theological Seminary, and the Gileskirk School. He is the author of dozens of books in the areas of history, biography, politics, literature, and social criticism. In addition to his regular classes in history, literature, theology, and the arts, he maintains an active writing and speaking schedule in this country and around the world. Information about his work and ministry may be found on his web site, www.KingsMeadow.com. He makes his home near Nashville, Tennessee, with his wife and children.